Praise for *Pha*

D1040042

"In all our efforts to live as committed believers, have we missed the very presence of God? Peter Haas's pointed and poignant question is long overdue. Using crafted storytelling and quick wit, he cuts to the heart of what it truly means and looks like to live a grace-centered life. Pharisectomy *offers much-needed insight for the church."*

—**Lindy Lowry**
Editor of *Outreach Magazine*

"It's hard to see our own hypocrisy in the mirror. Peter's book not only helps you identify it but eliminate it. Pharisectomy *explores the American church in an intriguing, entertaining, and insightful way."*

—**Craig Groeschel**
Senior pastor of LifeChurch.tv (Edmond, OK)
and author of *WEIRD: Because Normal Isn't Working*

"When trying to live righteously becomes a way to earn God's acceptance instead of being a response to His love, it can do much more harm than good. The Bible tells us salvation can't be earned . . . it's a free gift. Peter's life and this book are both compelling evidence of the powerful things God can do with someone who receives His free gift of grace. The book contains truths that can radically change your life!"

—**Robert Morris**
Senior pastor of Gateway Church (Southlake, TX)

"Pharisectomy *is one 'ectomy' that won't leave you in pain and discomfort but in joy, hope, humor, and renewed zest for life. One word of warning: the book is not your best airplane companion. You will disturb your seatmates by the laughter, the nodding of the head and, yes, the squirming—not to mention the puzzled interrogations about the title."*

—**Leonard Sweet**
Best-selling author, chief contributor to *sermons.com*, and professor
(Drew University and George Fox University)

"Truth be told, we all have a Pharisee inside us that we're reluctant to find. Through vulnerable stories, quick wit, bite-sized chapters, and challenging applications, Peter Haas helps us—from seasoned Christians to new ones— hop up on the operating table to have our inner Pharisee removed."

—Warren Bird
Research Director for Leadership Network
and author of *Multisite Roadtrip,*
Viral Churches, and *The Other 80%*

"God has given Peter Haas the ability to slap you in the face and hug you all at the same time! He is a voice of the new generation in the church world today. And he has something to say! Peter's humor and ultra practical insights make this book a must read."

—Matt Keller
Lead pastor of Next Level Church (Ft. Myers, FL)
and founder of Next Level Coaching (*www.MyNextLevel.me*)

"Peter Haas doesn't try to be relevant—he just is! Refreshingly authentic, his whimsical character should not be mistaken for shallowness. Pharisectomy can help cut out the legalism and religiosity without abandoning biblical righteousness and abiding spirituality."

—Rob Hoskins
President of OneHope, Inc.

"Peter's observations of the weird things churches do are hilarious yet painfully true. I actually found a few characters he described in my own church, and I hope they read this book too."

—Craig Altman
Senior pastor of Grace Family Church (Lutz, FL)

"Peter Haas is a fresh voice for the church and today's generation. I believe this book will be well received by some, a real challenge for others, and a two-by-four between the eyes for others. Read it, enjoy it, and see what God says to you while you listen to the stories Peter shares!"

—Rob Ketterling
Senior pastor of River Valley Church (Apple Valley, MN)

PHARISECTOMY

PHARISECTOMY

*How to Joyfully Remove Your Inner
Pharisee and Other Religiously
Transmitted Diseases*

by

Peter Haas

www.InfluencesResources.com

Copyright © 2012 by Peter Haas
ALL RIGHTS RESERVED

Published by Influence Resources
1445 N. Boonville Ave., Springfield, Missouri 65802

Published in association with The Quadrivium Group—Orlando, FL
info@TheQuadriviumGroup.com
Developmental Editing—Ben Stroup, BenStroup.com—Greenbrier, TN
Copy Editing and Proofreading—Kyle Olund, KLO Publishing—
Hendersonville, TN

ISBN: 978-1-93669-944-5
First printing 2012
Printed in United States of America

To my friend and mentor
Billy Hornsby (1949–2011)
You showed me that treating people with grace and
respect is one of the highest forms of worship.

Contents

Foreword

Let me start by saying that I love Peter Haas. I love his wit, I love his insight, I love his transparency. My life is better for having met him. I loved the title of this book when he first shared it with me. I had one of those "Why didn't I think of that?" moments.

So, why should you read it?

Have you ever run into someone who was totally cynical about church? They were fed up with the hypocrisy, the fighting, the legalism, and everything else in between. Maybe they were hurt by believers when they were young. Or maybe they tried to give church a chance at one point in their lives, only to find out that there was little love or acceptance to be found. The truth is, I think that anyone who has grown up in church can relate to those sorts of feelings. I can remember a time when I wondered if I wanted to be a part of the church any longer. I had been so turned off by fighting and ugliness that I wasn't sure it was worth it. Fortunately, God brought some good people into my life who reminded me that the church can also be a place of love and healing. Cynicism isn't just a problem for outsiders—those of us who have the most experience with church are sometimes the most cynical and bitter of all.

That is why I am excited about the book you are now reading. Peter knows all about those cynical feelings and what they can do to a person. Growing up, Peter experienced many different church denominations and styles, but came away with one basic assumption: church is a place you endure to keep God happy. Peter left the church with no intention of going back. Fortunately, God had other plans! A remarkable encounter with God in a nightclub convinced Peter to give religion (and church) a second chance, and he has never looked back. Like me, Peter is passionate to reach those who are unchurched or have left the church. Young people are leaving the church in droves, and I cannot think of a better person to bring them back than Peter.

Did I mention Peter is funny? Really funny. Years ago a mentor of mine told me that the secret of a good sermon is to "Make 'em laugh, make 'em cry, and give 'em Jesus." Peter's book definitely has the first one covered, and probably the second too. As for the third part, *Pharisectomy* helps the reader encounter Jesus in new and refreshing ways. This is a book for people who have been burned by church and for people who have never set foot inside a church. Peter knows what it is like to be both an insider and an outsider, which makes him uniquely able to speak to both groups. *Pharisectomy* is also a book for people who have been in church their whole lives but feel that many of their most basic questions have never been answered.

At its core, *Pharisectomy* is about dealing with the hypocrisy, the cynicism, and the elitism—not in others, but in ourselves. Peter does an excellent job of showing legalism for what it is and demonstrating just how dangerous it is. In many cases, legalism is the reason people have been hurt in churches and have no desire to return. But Peter shows that when we move past our bitterness and cynicism, we can experience the love, joy, and freedom Jesus has for us.

If you have ever been hurt in a church, or even if you were the one doing the hurting, I believe that this book has the potential to radically impact your life. A Pharisectomy is kind of like all those immunization shots you got when you were young—if you are going to be healthy, you need them. A Pharisectomy is an operation that all of us need, and I am grateful that Peter is here to walk us through the procedure.

—**Greg Surratt**
Lead pastor, Seacoast Church
and author of *Ir-Rev-Rend*

INTRODUCTION

Jesus Still Goes to Nightclubs

What might I need to know to survive this book?

Dɪᴅ ʏᴏᴜ ᴋɴᴏᴡ Jᴇsᴜs ɢᴏᴇs ᴛᴏ nightclubs? I'm not implying that He literally shows up and starts dancing. But in the Gospels, He certainly hung out in scandalous places. And He definitely came to *my* nightclub one night.

Believe it or not, I actually turned my life over to Christ while working as a rave DJ. I wasn't exactly open to Christianity at the time. So as you'd imagine, the story leading up to it is actually quite bizarre.

You should know I never actually *hated* Christians. I never really knew any of the "mean and restrictive" types (you know ... the ultra-conservative ones who worried that dancing might lead to premarital hand holding or that rock music, when played backward, tempted kids to watch the Smurfs).

Don't get me wrong. I knew those Christians existed, because their "Praise the Lord!" T-shirts gave them away. And someone was obviously passionate enough to scratch "I love Jesus" on the toilet stall at the local gas station, which struck me as an odd evangelism strategy. But their only real influence on our community was that they kept jean jumpers perpetually in style.

You see, where I grew up, church affiliation was nothing more than fire insurance. Almost everyone was Catholic or liberal protestant. Some of the best drinking parties of the year were actually fundraisers for local churches. Despite our families' libertarian stances on many things, no one seemed to have fun in church.

One time, I was at my grandma's church when suddenly an old man died in the pew in front of me. He kind of just tipped over in the middle

> *The whole experience came to symbolize my entire perception of church, a place where you endure boring rituals to keep God happy.*

of the sermon. Nobody seemed to react with urgency. Believe it or not, the service never stopped while the paramedics hauled the guy away! It was as though this sort of thing happened all the time. So I'm quite certain his autopsy showed he was officially bored to death. The whole experience came to symbolize my entire perception of church, a place where you endure boring rituals to keep God happy.

To make church services harder for me, my dad was passionately tone deaf in a crowd, and my mom was always the loudest and most enthusiastic harmonizer in the entire congregation. I secretly hoped that the organist would show up drunk one day and start randomly playing *Take Me Out to the Ball Game* or, at the very least, plunk out the cue for everyone to shout "Charge!"

Maybe the pipe organ itself was half of my problem. You see, I always thought it would be a perfect worship instrument if your middle name was Count Dracula or Phantom of the Opera. But for daily use, organs are a bit odd, don't you think? Have you ever been at a party and thought, "Man, if only we had a pipe organ? Let's get this party started!" Besides, I always thought it was strange that both haunted houses and churches endorsed the same favorite instrument. And when people literally died in front of me, this connection wasn't lost on me.

To be fair, I also didn't want a contemporary church either, because *contemporary worship* in my church dictionary generally meant *American Idol* for fifty-year-olds. My mom had a few melodramatic moments where she threatened to switch our family to one such church. We called them holy-roller churches. People did awkward things there that they didn't seem to do anywhere else. Everyone had their hands in the air as though they all spontaneously started to slow dance with a ten-foot Jesus. I felt like I was at a high school dance where everyone was slathering "invisible Jesus" with embarrassing public displays of affection. Not to mention the services were a good forty minutes longer. I concluded that most of us preferred a short

People did awkward things there that they didn't seem to do anywhere else. Everyone had their hands in the air as though they all spontaneously started to slow dance with a ten-foot Jesus.

and boring church experience rather than a long and uncomfortable love fest.

When I went to my liberal Lutheran confirmation class, I vividly remember my thirteen-year-old friend telling me on our extremely long trip to the bathroom, "If we can simply survive confirmation, we'll get to graduate from church." It sounded like such a poetic goal. "And it's awesome 'cuz grandma gives you money, and our moms won't force us to go to church anymore."

We were like two jailbirds watching the sun set on the wall of our dungeon. "Think of it this way," he consoled me, "it could be far worse. We could be stuck in a Catholic CCD class or one of those conservative churches where you never get to graduate." At the time it seemed like such a positive and inspirational outlook. After his halftime speech, I breathed in deeply through wide nostrils and set about my goal of graduating from church.

My Catholic friend, who was later kicked out of his CCD classes, kept encouraging us to follow his lead. But I didn't quite have the guts to snort holy water up my nose like he did. Besides, Lutherans don't have holy water. Nonetheless, I almost succeeded in getting kicked out one Wednesday night service during Lent.

It was already hard enough to attend on Sundays, but going on Wednesdays during Lent was torture. Fortunately, I got to sit with my friend on Wednesday nights. But we were a terrible combination. In an attempt to entertain ourselves, we discovered that it's possible to blow out a candle that's twelve feet away, such as the candles on the altar in the front of the church.

So during Communion one Wednesday, we knelt down near the altar with the intent of achieving this feat. Of course, the trick was to blow without looking conspicuous. And if you closed your eyes while blowing, it looked like you were extremely passionate, perhaps relieved, about receiving Communion. Then after a mind-numbing, hilarious, four-second delay, the candles would suddenly cower under our pubescent manliness.

The thought never occurred to us that half the audience was watching. In a Pentecostal church, our heavy "Communion breathing" might have passed suspicion, but Lutheran boys simply aren't that passionate about wine and wafers. Our confirmation teacher was furious. But unlike our local nuns, my Lutheran educators were so filled with grace that we weren't successful in getting kicked out. It seemed we were in it for the long haul.

THE NIGHT JESUS WENT CLUBBING

I, ultimately, succeeded in my goal of graduating from church. And from that point on, I simply did what most young people do—I experimented with everything. Quitting church enabled me to stay up incredibly late going to nightclubs. I eventually became a rave DJ. Before long, I was mixing and scratching up unsavory dance mixes and selling them all over the place.

As cool as it sounds, it was a miserable season of my life. Although I was free from church, I was empty inside. I was dating my future wife at the time. One day, she discovered her father's body after he committed suicide in their backyard. That same week, my good friend died in a car accident. So like most people when they're confronted with their mortality, I started to ask questions about the deep things of life.

I knew enough to know that this entire world couldn't have just spontaneously arrived out of nothing. A Christian friend once told me, "When you ask God to reveal Himself to you, He will." But I kept telling myself, "Been there. Done that." On the other hand, Atheism felt like an equally blind and ignorant reaction to Christianity. One night while at the nightclub where I was working, I got so depressed that I did an extremely scary thing . . . I prayed.

Praying felt a lot like wearing lederhosen. If you're not familiar with these stylish yet traditional European suspender-shorts, you should know that wearing them makes you feel like churning butter and dancing. The ethnic dress code somehow connects you with your heritage yet simultaneously makes you wonder if it's just another effeminate thing your mother talked you into doing. Put that together, and that's what that prayer felt like to me.

As I stood in the DJ booth on the second story of this nightclub and looked down, I noticed everyone was drunk, stoned, or aimless. I just felt overwhelmed with sadness for the first time. And out of my mouth leapt this prayer, "God, whoever you are . . . whatever you are . . . if you were powerful enough to create the world, then you should be powerful enough to reveal yourself to me. Show me the right religion, and I'll follow you. Give me a sign."

I was hoping for lightning bolts across the sky spelling out: Islam, Buddhism, or "None of the Above." Suddenly, I snapped out of my deep prayer and thought, "What am I doing?" as I became conscious of my lederhosen. "Am I praying? Wow. I need a cigarette." So I passed things off to my assistant and headed for the door.

Only a few steps away from the stairwell, a total stranger approached me. At first I thought he was trying to sell me drugs. I missed most of his first statement with the blaring music. But his next statement rattled me to the core. He said, "Jesus wants you to follow Him!"

"What did you say?" Perhaps I didn't hear him correctly. Getting closer to him, he repeated, "Jesus has a plan for your life, and He wants you to follow Him. If you follow Him, He'll give you a buzz like you've never experienced before."

Suddenly, I came to the terrifying realization that *just maybe* God had heard my prayer. I mean, what are the odds? I just prayed this heartfelt prayer thirty seconds earlier. And now, moments later, Jesus is literally taking over strange people in my nightclub. Much like Agent Smith in the *Matrix*, it seemed like Jesus could, at will, take over anyone's body in that entire place to stop me. I was cornered and scared out of my mind.

The words just flew out of my mouth, "Tell me what I'm supposed to do!" At first, the young Jesus-man looked at me as if I was mocking him, but I wasn't joking one bit. I was spooked. God had answered my call. I sure as heck better pay attention and respond.

The guy stammered confusingly about what to do next. "Uh . . . well . . . uh . . . I guess we could pray?" So right there in the nightclub, I prayed this old-fashioned repentance prayer. I really had no idea about what I was entering into.

This strange, young man begged me to meet him at church the next morning. Even after I woke up, I was still a bit spooked over how quickly God had answered my prayer. I grabbed my stuff and headed off to church. Looking back, it's still a bit crazy that I went. Of course, I stood out like a sore thumb with my grunge hair and Nine Inch Nails T-shirt. I was about to become baptized into every imaginable subculture of evangelical and charismatic Christianity.

Over the next few years, I checked out all sorts of churches. To my friends and family, it appeared as though I had fallen off the deep end. And in many ways, I had. Although I had spent years making fun of evangelical and charismatic church culture, I secretly felt that God's response to my nightclub prayer demanded that I try out every weird part of Christianity for a season. And this book documents a few of those funniest moments.

Most Christians are completely blind to their subculture. As you'll see throughout this book, the church is filled with unique assumptions about life that don't even come from the Bible. And if you've grown up in church, I hope this book will give you fresh eyes into the reality that many Americans find themselves in. Like me, they've quit on church. And the stats are rather staggering.

Although around 43 percent of Americans claim to go to church, only about 17 to 20.4 percent actually went to church last weekend.[1] That's to any kind of church, including ones where the gospel may be absent or hard to find. If you parse that number down to those

Bottom line, churches are failing to connect, and it has become an epidemic. Church, as we have known it, simply isn't working.

who actually attended "evangelical or charismatic" churches, some put that number as low as 9.1 percent, the majority of whom are baby boomers or senior citizens.[2] That means, most of the young people in America have quit on church.[3] One scholar noted that there's not a single state in the U.S., except Hawaii, where evangelical or charismatic church growth even kept pace with population growth since 1990.[4] Bottom line, churches are failing to connect, and it has become an epidemic. Church, as we have known it, simply isn't working.

These stats drove me into church leadership. I had hoped my outsider perspective might offer me some valuable insight. Within a relatively short period of time, I became a youth pastor with thousands of people coming to our youth ministry events. Honestly, I can't take credit for any of my early ministry successes. God clearly had me on a fast track. Stranger still, by my mid-twenties, I ended up taking over the church where I began as a youth pastor.

Becoming a senior pastor automatically turns you into a magnet for weird Christian agendas, especially when you're taking over a church. I wasn't quite ready to hear the deluge of spiritual critiques that most pastors deal with. In some ways, pastoring a church is like competing in an extreme sport where you run through a dense pack of grizzly bears every Sunday. On one hand, it's a rush. On the other hand, you quickly become aware of just how hostile a church environment can be.

And to be fair, I quickly realized that I was inadvertently "punching grizzly bears" by being naïve to Christian taboos. As you'll discover in upcoming chapters, I did everything a good pastor isn't supposed to do. For example, I once cussed in the pulpit (with good intensions, of course). My wife was probably the first pastor's wife in America to have her nose pierced. I also played card games other than UNO. And worst of all, I once confessed in the pulpit that Halloween was my favorite holiday, which is basically the first step in converting to Satanism.

Thankfully, the majority of the people in that church were both healthy and merciful on me as I grew up in front of them. And after a decade of untamed leadership lessons, we moved several hours away to plant a new church community called Substance in Minneapolis. And that is where the five of us (me and my wife, plus three kids) currently call home.

THE ART OF PHARISECTOMY

Now after hearing my story, it probably wouldn't be a stretch for you to believe that Substance is a pretty unusual church. Many people talk about our fast growth, our video campuses, and our ability to do an all techno worship set. But what really makes us unique is the people we attract. Believe it or not, over 70 percent of the thousands who show up are under age thirty, and few of them have ever been a part of a church before. Indeed, our fastest-growing campus is in a county where less than 5.1 percent of the population goes to *any* evangelical or charismatic church of *any* kind.

Although we get a few "Christian transfers" from other churches, we tend to get a really eclectic mix—from liberal professors to drug dealers—even people involved with organized crime. Almost every Sunday, I talk to young professionals who are still hung over from the night before. I constantly remind our volunteers, "Don't assume that you know what a meth addict looks like." In fact, it's not uncommon for visitors to call me *Father Peter* for lack of a better expression. (I have to admit that my three kids used to get really confused by this. They would say, "Daddy . . . do you really have other kids? . . . and why are they so old?")

People like this don't stay very long in a place with religious diseases.

In fact, last month I talked to a thirty-five-year-old who had literally never said the word *pastor* in his entire life. So stories like these have had a big influence on why I'm writing this book, because people like this don't stay very long in a place with religious diseases.

Much of this book is written for them. Like me, they are starting a strange new journey into the jungles of Western Christianity. And like me, they will encounter all sorts of misguided approaches to God. Thus, I want to be the fun-loving tour guide who points out religious diseases before they contract one. My hope is you'll join me on this adventure.

Parts of our journey will answer basic questions like: If we're forgiven, then why do we use guilt to motivate ourselves and others? or How do Christians get so mean? But things will get very interesting once we ask questions like: What does biblical legalism really look like? and What would a Pharisee look like today?

As we study a few of their characteristics, you're going to see a lot of things about Western Christianity in a whole new light. Some of you are finally going to be able to put a finger on why you gave up on church. Others will discover how to become a tour guide like me, a person who helps others stay in the life-giving joy of Christ. But before we venture out, it's important for me to establish a few ground rules.

Requirement #1: Keep a Sense of Humor

Keep in mind I have a severe allergy to overly serious books. For example, have you ever read a Christian book that just makes you want to hate everything about the church, the Bride of Christ? I call them "Bride-hater" books. Their strategy is to get Christians so revved up about the church that we'll suddenly "hate it" back into improvement. (By the way, I tried this technique on my wife once; it didn't go well.) So we'll take a more tongue-in-cheek approach to things.

We're going to talk about chain-smoking monkeys and illegal uses of underwear. There are some unusual things in Christianity, and we are going to have some fun with them.

But we'll also talk about serious things, like the time when God performed an undeniable miracle in front of us or the time when God recently called me to completely empty almost all of my financial savings and bank accounts for His kingdom. So there will be conviction mixed with frankly entertaining stories. And somehow, amidst this curious mix of seemingly unrelated items, we will grasp a profound new way of relating to God, a non-Pharisee way of being a God follower.

As the book goes on, I'm going to get increasingly deep. Like a doctor checking for prostate cancer, I'm going to put a finger in, and on, some things. And it might get a little bit awkward. (I'm feeling awkward already, aren't you?) You see, we're going to explore the hidden priorities and assumptions that many churches operate with. So I hope you keep sledding through the rest of this book. I proudly avoided having any filler in this book. And many of my nerdy friends tell me that I've kept the best for last.

Requirement #2: Don't Let Your Youngsters Read This Book

Keep in mind, this book is definitely rated PG-13. I share fascinating statistics about how church attendance affects sexual satisfaction amidst other eye-opening details. Thus, it might cause your *tweenager* to ask you some potentially complicated (or at least out of the ordinary) questions. Thankfully, I won't have to be there if this happens. But there's one last thing.

Requirement #3: Don't Use This Book to Judge the Weird Church Down the Street

A while back I was driving on a six-lane interstate in Minneapolis. People were driving terribly. And there was this clueless dork in front of me who left his blinker on. Finally, he turned it off. Next thing you know, there's another idiot who left his blinker on. And for a guy like me who prides himself on his self-awareness, a rant suddenly leapt out of my mouth like a roaring tiger, "Can you believe all of these stupid drivers? What is wrong with everybody?" And right before I finished, I looked down to a horrifying revelation: *I* was the one who had his blinker on. In fact, *they* were signaling *me*.

Likewise, most of the people who have religiously transmitted diseases don't even realize they have them. Ironically, you can have religious diseases and not even be going to church right now. Quite often, the people who are most cynical about the church are the ones who've contracted the greatest number of religious diseases.

> *Most of the people who have religiously transmitted diseases don't even realize they have them.*

I regularly run into a lot of young Christians who like to imagine themselves as totally disease-free. "I'm not like my parents or that weird church down the road," they say. Other Christians falsely think that by attending a hip, non-traditional church they are suddenly exempt from religiously transmitted diseases. Not true. As you'll soon find out, postmodern hipster-Christians often have an equal number of religious diseases as the boring, traditional ones.

Truth be told, we *all* have a hidden Pharisee lurking inside us. Besides, there's nothing worse than ignorantly driving through life with your blinker on. How sad would it be if we spent most of our lives bickering at the very saints who were trying to help us the most?

So hop onto the operating table. My stories will be both absurd and true. And I promise to keep things light-hearted. (I won't make you wear lederhosen, even though that would be fun.) And hopefully I haven't already offended any of you pipe organ lovers. There's actually a small place in my heart that still enjoys one played (a very, very small place).

But no matter where you're at in your faith journey, open up your heart to God. After all, He's a real prankster. And He just might show up in *your* nightclub.

> *Truth be told, we* all *have a hidden Pharisee lurking inside us.*

CHAPTER ONE

How I Became an Urban Legend

What are the fundamentals of a modern-day Pharisee?

THE FIRST TIME I EVER CUSSED into a church microphone was right after I became a youth pastor. I'm not saying it was the best decision. I've always been an odd fit for pastoring. But the kids dug my exceptionally long hair, especially in a Pentecostal church. I looked as though I had just quit an intense grunge band. So the church folk were genuinely afraid that my alternative looks might lead their teens astray. They wrote letters and informed the hierarchy that "long hair on guys is the precursor to premarital sex." I had spent many rebellious years hoping this was true, but to no avail. Despite my suspicious looks, my senior pastor was super-cool and willing to accept the risks and the critique letters over a hire like me, which makes the following story ten times funnier.

I was preaching from the New Testament where Paul starts ripping on his previous approaches toward God. He compared all of his former Pharisaical ways to dung or rubbish in light of the "surpassing greatness of knowing Christ" (Phil. 3:8). Of course, being fresh out of my college Greek class, I started explaining to my pubescent crowd that the words *dung* or *rubbish* weren't an adequate translation. Paul used a far grittier word. So to climax my riveting exegesis, I proceeded to translate Paul in a way they would never forget.

"Young people, he's actually sayin' that his entire world outside of Christ, including his religiosity, was nothing more than a pile of S#*!" A wide-eyed hush swept across the crowd. As crickets chirped, the eighth graders looked on, bewildered yet smiling ear to ear. Then, in what I imagined to be anointed passion, I repeated the official Peter Haas Translation (PHT) a few more ways.

To add to my foible, the youth ministry auditorium shared a thin wall with about a half dozen children's classrooms. With every choice word, hundreds of sweet little kids went wide-eyed and slack-jawed on the other side of the dividing wall.

At the time, I was too impressed with my biblical insights to consider the implications of my new PA system. Every time the Sunday school teachers reeled their kids back into their Bible lesson on Noah, a booming new S-bomb would drop. Noah's Ark was a sunken ship. Everyone was wondering what that scary, new youth pastor was doing over there.

Needless to say, after barely surviving a mob of concerned parents, I almost lost my job. As my pastor graciously listened to me explain myself, I protested, "But more people gave their lives to Christ in that service than we've ever seen in our ministry." The ministry that had spanned only three months, mind you. Much like a person standing in front of a television judge on a courtroom show, I suddenly became uncomfortably aware of how ridiculous my argument was becoming. Quite ironically, I was up a "certain creek" without a paddle. So I did what any self-respecting, hyper-spiritual person would do; I played the God-card.

"God told me to do it," I exclaimed. At the time it seemed like a novel argument that nobody had ever thought of before. My pastor graciously let me off the hook after a much needed tongue-lashing. He also told me to alert him if "God told me" to do anything else. But I guarantee you that none of those youngsters will ever forget Philippians 3. None of us should, because it is significant. Despite my imperfect exposition, Paul is still saying something quite scandalous. He was a Pharisee, yet he rejected this approach to God for something totally new.

The Pharisees were a well-respected group of people. After two thousand years of demonizing them, we forget the fact that many people saw them as the apex of spirituality. They were a religious revival, a "back to the Bible" movement. It was a holiness movement mixed with charismatic prayer. Many Pharisees memorized all of the Pentateuch, the first five books of the Bible. It wasn't unusual for Pharisees to pray and meditate for nine hours every day in three, three-hour segments. Many would also fast for two entire days each week. So these guys were no slouches when it came to spiritual discipline. And yet, both Paul and Jesus are scandalously saying their approach to God is actually missing it.

Now if you were trying to peg Jesus as belonging to a certain group, He probably would have fit in best with the Pharisees. Ironically, the Sadducees, Essenes, and other contemporaries were in many ways more legalistic and dysfunctional than their Pharisaic counterparts. And, yes, the Gospels repeatedly refer to the Pharisees as a nemesis of sorts to Jesus (Matt. 16:12; Matt. 23). Even though Jesus didn't subscribe to many of their purity rituals (Mark 7), He definitely substantiated much of their theological worldviews (Matt. 23:2–3).[5] However, Jesus distinguished an approach to God that was sensationally unique, even to the Pharisees.

But first, it's important to understand that within Pharisaical circles, there were two main schools of thought. Some belonged to the school of Shammai, the name of their popular teacher. His interpretations of the Law were notorious for being extra stringent. Thus, it was said that Shammai required a "heavy yoke," a large list of do's and don'ts in order to be a healthy God-follower. Even today, every pastor and church has a yoke of sorts, a statement of faith or an unspoken list of behaviors that needs to be followed. For example, swearing in the pulpit is usually a no-no in most churches. (I know! It's shocking but true.)

Jesus distinguished an approach to God that was sensationally unique, even to the Pharisees.

In contrast, the Pharisaical school of Hillel was a bit more relaxed and liberal. But even Hillel advocated a yoke that would make all of us look like scrawny wimps. Indeed, the Pharisees were so obsessed with maintaining their ceremonial purity that they'd rarely even eat with a normal person (aka a non-Pharisee). They'd even make all of their incoming adherents practice techniques on how to avoid touching a non-Pharisee's clothing out of fear of defiling themselves. Even relaxed Pharisaical schools would require new trainees to maintain mind-blowing levels of ritual purity for three months to a year before granting them full acceptance.

Despite the passion and zeal with which these groups studied and applied Scripture, it's interesting that Jesus didn't solidly join any of these groups. Certainly, this must have been peculiar to His first-century listeners. In fact, in total contrast to many of His Pharisaical comparisons, Christ said, ". . . my yoke is easy and my burden is light" (Matt. 11:30). He is saying that His approach to spirituality is incredibly simple. My list of dos and don'ts is refreshingly shorter than most. Indeed, Jesus went as far as to say that following God should be virtually effortless and joy-filled, even during tough times and difficult moments.

Matthew 13:44 is one of my favorite descriptions of Christianity. Jesus said, "The kingdom of heaven is like a treasure hidden in a field. When a man found it, he hid it again, and then in his joy went and sold all he had and bought that field." In other words, when a person has a true encounter with God (the treasure), they'll do anything to possess it. Anything that stands in the way (e.g., sin) is joyfully set aside.

And notice the man in this parable didn't sell all that he had reluctantly or under compulsion. He didn't say, "Ugh! Christianity is so tough!" He didn't sit around and grieve. He didn't do it because someone logically argued him into it or because it was the right thing

Indeed, Jesus went as far as to say that following God should be virtually effortless and joy-filled, even during tough times and difficult moments.

to do. He did it joyfully because he knew he had just won the lottery.

The Bible isn't a list of requirements; rather, it's a list of results after experiencing God's love.

Paul later writes that it is God's kindness that leads us toward repentance (Rom. 2:4). This means any repentance that isn't a reaction to God's treasure is false repentance, which is precisely what diseased believers miss.

Quite often, the advocates of dead religion bid us to take up crosses without preaching a joy set before us (Heb. 12:2). Rather than helping people experience the treasure firsthand, they simply shame people into buying it or expect people to take their word for it, as if a theoretical description should suffice.

Yet Paul rejected these approaches saying, "My message and my preaching were not with wise and persuasive words, but with a demonstration of the Spirit's power, so that your faith might not rest on men's wisdom, but on God's power" (1 Cor. 2:4–5). Even Paul understood that if people don't experience the treasure firsthand, then obedience will feel forced and unnatural.

And that's a perfect description of pharisaical faith, an obligation to serve God that's instilled through guilt or logic. Sadly, many Christians are about as happy as a bag of rocks when it comes to things of faith.

So before diving into the rest of this book, it's critical that I make one simple truth loud and clear: The Bible isn't a list of requirements; rather, it's a list of results after experiencing God's love. Following God isn't an action but a reaction. And if you have to painstakingly motivate yourself or others to serve God "because it's the right thing to do," you've already missed the very foundations of biblical Christianity.

Unfortunately, many churches peddle joyless obligation as though it was God's greatest gift. The results of this approach can be exceptionally destructive.

Pharisaical faith is a lot like threatening your kids at a sports game, "When our team scores a touchdown, you better cheer or I will spank you! And, doggone it little Bobby, you better give them a whoop-whoop or, so help me, I will give you a whoop-whoop." Unfortunately, many churches peddle joyless obligation as though it was God's greatest gift. The results of this approach can be exceptionally destructive.

A RIVERDANCER HAVING A STROKE

Not long after I gave my life to Christ, I visited many small Pentecostal and evangelical churches throughout the region. Everything about these churches was weird to me. But after Christ answered that prayer of mine in that nightclub, I felt like I needed to embrace His people no matter how bizarre they were. One such church experience made me question my open-minded approach, though. The moment the service started, it turned into a freak-fest like I had never seen before.

Like most Americans, I had never really been in a contemporary worshiping church before. Seeing people raise their hands in worship was already mind-blowing to me. But this church was on a whole new level.

The moment the first chord was struck, flags and banners exploded out of nowhere. Imagine a fireworks show in the backseat of your car. The previously normal-looking woman next to me suddenly sprung into a shocking gyration with her ribbons. She looked like a cross between Kevin Bacon in *Footloose* and an amateur ninja practicing twirling kicks.

At one point, her ribbon accidently whipped me in the eye like a towel snap in a gym shower. She didn't even notice that I had almost lost my eye. She probably assumed that I was crying out of joy.

To make matters worse, a large man in front of me kept unsuccessfully trying to blow into a shofar horn. In between blows he would wheeze. It sounded like a dying moose call. In my heart I kept rooting for him, "You can do it! Take a deeper breath." But despite the strangeness of it all, I kept thinking to myself, "What do I know about God? Maybe I'm missing out?" Besides, were my all-night rave parties really that different? But then something happened that made me rethink everything.

I was still a new believer. I had been naïvely dragging all of my pot-smoking friends to church. One of my friends was already a bit concerned about my eye wound. So when the band broke into this unique two-step song that seemed to cross polka music with the opening number from *Fiddler on the Roof*, my friend stressfully blurted, "Bro, I really need a smoke." Just before he escaped, the worship leader started yelling, "Come on people! Dance like David danced! If you loved God, you'd be dancing right now." Amazingly, he then started pointing out people in the audience who weren't "giving their all to Christ" in dance.

I began feeling totally condemned at this point. If I didn't start doing the Pentecostal two-step kick, I was pretty sure that I was going straight to hell. Yet my friend, who had already accepted the fact he's going to hell, wasn't about to move a muscle. So I was conflicted. I wanted to demonstrate normalcy to my invited friend; yet, I simultaneously didn't want the earth to open up and swallow me in a fiery blaze. Suddenly, the left side of my body—the side that was opposite my unchurched friend—started dancing, and my right side tried to stand as stoic and uninterested as possible. I probably looked like a Riverdancer having a stroke. But what was I supposed to do?

The sad part was, despite all the hype, there was no real joy in the room. I've been at parties when my team won the Super Bowl. We went crazy. But this service was a faint echo of that passing joy. Yet true worship should feel a million times better than a silly football game! And it wasn't the flags, ribbons, or ninja-like twirling that bothered me. Because after a long hard day, a few ninja twirls might feel exhilarating. Rather, it was the inauthenticity of the whole thing. It was contrived. Even worse, it was induced and obligatory. And if I, as a baby Christian, could feel the inauthenticity, no wonder God Himself looks at the heart and not the format

(1 Sam. 16:7). If only Christians would do the same.

This worship leader used guilt and peer pressure to create the pretense for passionate worship, at least as that church defined it. And

Biblical repentance is a reaction to God's kindness, not an action to earn it.

guilt can be a powerful motivator, which is why people use it. That only works for a season.

That's why the Bible offers us a far more powerful motivator: unmerited grace. Again, biblical repentance is a reaction to God's kindness, not an action to earn it (Rom. 2:4). Righteousness is not the reward of living rightly. It's the unmerited gift that irresistibly results in right living (Titus 3:5). Or as Paul puts it, "For the grace of God . . . teaches us to say 'No' to ungodliness," not guilt, shame, or clever manipulation techniques (Titus 2:11–12).

So here's a simple way to assess yourself: If you think that serving God is hard or oppressive, chances are you have false repentance lurking in your heart. If the process of getting sin out of your life is anything but joyful, then chances are you have never experienced the true treasure in the first place. If you did, then perhaps you have since abandoned it for a works-oriented faith. And now you're an action, not a reaction.

If this is you, listen closely to me. Because if you continue living in this false religion, you're not only going to get more confused but you'll confuse others, which is probably how you got suckered into thinking Christian obedience is joyless in the first place.

You see, despite everything Paul achieved as a Pharisee, he considered all of it dung compared to the surpassing greatness of knowing Christ. Why? Because Paul found a treasure that changes everything—motivation included.

But have you found this treasure? If you're still a bit confused by this new approach to God, allow me to reveal one final contrast between Jesus and His religious contemporaries.

HOW TO MAKE JESUS MAD

In John 4, we read about Jesus having a conversation with a Samaritan woman. Jews hated Samaritans, so it's quite radical that Jesus, a Jew, would even have a conversation with her, let alone talk to a woman of her reputation. Just when she was being reeled into Christ's winsome ways, she put her guard up and started giving Him a classic worship debate.

"You Jews claim that the place where we must worship is in Jerusalem" (John 4:20). In other words, you Jews reject us because you think we have compromised worship. But Jesus dismantled this entire way of thinking by saying, "Yet a time is coming and has now come when the true worshipers will worship the Father in spirit and truth, for they are the kind of worshipers the Father seeks" (John 4:23). In other words, if you think worship is a format, like where you worship, how many songs, or how much altar ministry, etc., then you've already missed God's heart. And why? Because worship is a heart condition, not a church formula or any other system that is created by men (Col. 2:8).

In fact, right after this conversation, Jesus started an unlikely revival in a place like Samaria that defied the appropriate worship formula of His day. It was almost as if He were saying, "The moment you try to create an elite worship formula, God is going to break out of it."

But with this story in mind, check out what Jesus said in Mark 11:15. It's the story where Jesus went into the temple and wildly overturned the tables of the money-changers. What in the world could make the Son of God so mad that He'd violently overturn tables? Believe it or not, this passage has nothing to do with prayer. In fact,

In other words, if you think worship is a format, like where you worship, how many songs, or how much altar ministry, etc., then you've already missed God's heart.

I believe that Jesus had the Samaritan woman in mind when He did this. So allow me to explain.

The Jews of Jerusalem liked to see themselves as having the purest form of worship. And in those days, many connected pure worship to a geographical location. Thus, as a message to outsiders, "real Jews" would make it hard for any travelers to come worship. After all, in order to worship, you needed a sacrifice of some sort. Yet the nature of travel in those days made it next to impossible to bring your own animals with you. Thus, in order to worship, travelers would have to spend inordinate amounts of money to purchase sacrificial animals at inflated costs to connect with God. This hurdle made it clear that true followers of God lived in Jerusalem. Like the Samaritan woman mentioned, Jerusalem was the holy city (John 4:20).

So let's look at the reason Jesus gave for overturning the tables. He quoted directly from Isaiah 56:7, where God says that "my house will be called a house of prayer for all nations." It's critical to understand Jesus' emphasis wasn't prayer. Jews were already constantly in prayer. Many Pharisees prayed for nine hours a day. So I highly doubt Jesus was suggesting increasing the total time in prayer to ten or twelve hours, as if there were some magical number that would suddenly satisfy God. Besides, Jesus' listeners would have instantaneously understood He was quoting Isaiah 56, which puts a profound spin on why Christ overturned tables.

In Isaiah 56, God also gives a pretty strong indictment of elitist spirituality. God goes out of His way to encourage outsiders, those who feel incompatible with the elitist approaches to true worship. God makes the case that He will defend those who the hyperspiritual world deems compromised. And arguably, Christ was the ultimate fulfillment of this.

Jesus was upset because religious people were trying to make God inaccessible to those outside

> *Jesus was upset because religious people were trying to make God inaccessible to those outside their approach to worship.*

their approach to worship. And worst of all, they were doing it under the guise of protecting true spirituality, even though they really didn't give a rip about the nations or those outside the temple walls. And unfortunately, modern-day Pharisees do the same thing.

Today, many Christians use music as the central driving force of the church service. Personally, I love this, yet music wasn't even used this way until Wesley or the Moravians in the 1700s. Some historians credit Charles Finney in the 1800s as being one of the first to design emotional worship experiences leading to altar ministry in the modern or charismatic sense. Thus, the modern concept of creating an extended musical worship or prayer experience is fairly new to Christianity. And yet, for many Christians, the music and altar ministry has idolatrously become the very litmus test as to whether the Holy Spirit even attends that church.

Please don't misunderstand me. I love powerful, Spirit-filled worship experiences. In fact, we regularly have worship nights that go on for several hours straight. At Substance, our church is filled with brilliant musicians, intercessors, and worshipers who love to go deep with God.

But I bring up this example to show that, quite often, we're really no different than the Pharisees. They spiritualized and idolized their purity rituals and temple procedures. So when Jesus didn't do worship in the exact way that they idealized, they couldn't even imagine Him as being a legit God-follower. Indeed, they missed the literal presence of God because He just didn't fit into their narrow concept of an anointed lifestyle. These same pharisaical tendencies are still alive and well.

That's why I get a little bit irked when Christians misinterpret Jesus' anger in the temple as being an argument for more intense prayer and worship. There's certainly a time for intense prayer and God-seeking. But in this passage, that's the exact opposite message that Jesus was trying to get across.

We need to become painfully aware of how we're obscuring God from those who need to connect with Him the most: the lost.

Instead, Jesus was arguing for a more accessible worship experience. We need to become painfully aware of how we're obscuring God from those who need to connect with Him the most: the lost. To be honest, I was one of those lost people. And if God hadn't miraculously ambushed me in that nightclub, I would have given up on church like most Americans.

THE URBAN LEGEND

So allow me to wind down by explaining where we're going in the next few chapters. There is a lot of spiritual sounding stuff in modern Christianity that still obscures people's ability to get in sync with God's true work on earth. In the coming chapters, I'm going to give you numerous test questions that will help you evaluate this for yourself. And hopefully it will prevent you from enrolling in the school of hard knocks. Fortunately, you can learn from my mistakes. And speaking of mistakes, there's a ridiculous part two to the story surrounding my "S-bomb Sermon."

At first I thought my infamous message would stay with me in Wisconsin. Seven years later I was attending a pastor's conference out West, a twenty-two hour drive from that church. A group of pastors and I were lamenting over the stupid things we've done in the pulpit. Suddenly, one of the pastors began, "But guys, nobody can top this story. I once heard about a pastor who was preaching on Philippians 3 and . . ." he started describing someone who did the exact same thing as me!

At first I thought, "Whew! I'm not alone in being an idiot." But as the story rolled on, it became clear that I was that man he was talking about. I was famous, but that is not something you want to be remembered for among your pastor friends. Sweat started pouring down my brow. I think at one point I confidently shouted, "What an idiot! . . . What was he thinking?" After all, it was a rather famous minister who was sharing the story.

And I'm not sure what happened next—whether I was in my body or out—but I vaguely remember confessing to my colleagues that I was that man. And now, three hundred therapy sessions later, I can laugh about it. Indeed, I'm quite proud of the fact that I'm an urban legend.

But I'm living proof that God can use anyone. He has a sense of humor. He has a joy that is greater than anything you can imagine. So stay on the operating table. This Pharisectomy is just getting started. Once you experience this change, it will be downright painful to ever return to lifeless religion again.

CHAPTER ONE IN REVIEW

Key Ideas

1. Religion is no substitute for an authentic relationship with God. This was the trap of the Pharisees.

2. Jesus' approach to spirituality is incredibly simple; His list of do's and don'ts is short.

3. When a person has a true encounter with God, he will do anything to possess it.

4. Many Christians today serve God out of a sense of obligation that is the result of guilt or misapplied logic.

5. God looks at the heart of our worship, not the format.

6. Grace is the unmerited gift that results in right living.

7. Often our attempts to protect the true message of the gospel actually obscure it.

8. Christians today are much like the Pharisees in that they spiritualize and idolize their rituals. They actually worship the worship service.

9. Worship often communicates little about God and a lot about us.

10. Lifeless religion has become the norm for many believers.

Discussion Questions

1. Was there any information about the Pharisees that was new or interesting to you? If so, what?

2. If you had a Christian upbringing, in your opinion, did you come from a tradition that advocated a "heavy" or "light" yoke? Give examples as to why you think this.

3. Matthew 13:44 teaches that the process of getting sin out of our lives should be joyful. Have you ever tried to obey God reluctantly or under obligation? How did this make you feel?

4. Grace is an unmerited gift that results in right living. What does your lifestyle say about the presence of God's grace in your life?

5. Think about your most recent worship experience. Was the focus more on people or on God? Explain how you know the answer.

6. How are you dealing with current sin-struggles that make you feel oppressed or joyless?

7. Have you ever been to a church with a strange worship format? How did you feel? Did you think the service was designed for believers or unbelievers?

8. Does worship at your church lead people toward a relationship with God, or is it an obstacle to seeing God for who He really is? Explain.

9. In your opinion, what are a few modern examples of how churches make it hard for outsiders to understand the gospel? Are there any worship practices that you love that might be hard for newcomers to enjoy? Why?

10. Based on what you read in this chapter, how will you approach worship differently?

Why I Gave Up on Chopping off Hands

Why don't we obey every rule in the Bible?

FOR A SEASON, MY WIFE AND I decided we would only play our audio Bible when we were in our car. Our hope was that our three kids would get a little extra exposure to Scripture. Of course, if you've ever read the whole Bible, you'll quickly realize that there are many parts that are definitely R-rated. I realized this the hard way as my nine-, seven-, and four-year-old kids heard the following passage one morning from Deuteronomy 25:11–12: "If two men are fighting and the wife of one of them comes to rescue her husband from his assailant, and she reaches out and seizes him by his private parts, you shall cut off her hand. Show her no pity."

My kids quickly realized that they weren't getting the whole story in their classes at church. None of my kids cared about Jonah or Goliath anymore. "Dad, can we read Deuteronomy again?" they'd continually say with a curious snicker.

I don't preach on this verse very often as it's only an occasional problem for my church. However, I am known to hold this verse up at football games and write it on sympathy cards, just to see if people actually read Scripture references.

But seriously, I was captivated when I first read this. Was it *that* big of a problem that God had to personally address it? Was there a rash of husky women crossing the line of appropriateness? I always imagined God reaching His breaking point, "That's it! Enough's enough! Whatever happened to a wholesome old-fashioned man-fight?"

But here's the real question I want to ponder: Why do modern Christians apply certain Old Testament commands like, "Do not steal" but not others like, "Cut off her hand"? I mean there are all sorts of unique Old Testament commands that we no longer apply.

As a young Christian, I wondered if we weren't being a bit hypocritical about which parts of the Bible we wanted to obey. Part of it was because I didn't understand Covenant Law very well. And, quite frankly, modern Pharisees still don't.

People would often say, "Well much of that Law passed away with the New Covenant." But this sweeping statement didn't really settle things for me. I think that most intellectually honest Christians are going to need a little more clarity. Theologian J. I. Packer proposed a solution for this confusion by distinguishing three separate types of Law (the lists of do's and don'ts that God gave to Moses): Moral, Civil/Political, and Ceremonial Law.[6]

Moral Law represents good things to do all the time. The Ten Commandments are no less relevant today than they were thousands of years ago. No Christian would kill their neighbor and say, "It's all good. I'm a New Testament Christian. I'm not under the Law, right?" And why not? Because these commands are generally good advice no matter what time period you live in.

The second type of Law in the Old Testament is Civil/Political Law. These laws were essentially an application of Moral Law on a municipal and national level. These are the Mosaic equivalent of speed limits and garbage restrictions. So if the Moral Law says, "Love your neighbor as yourself," then the Civil Law might say, "Don't practice on your shofar at 3 a.m." Most of these laws only applied as long as Israel was an autonomous nation-state.

> But this sweeping statement didn't really settle things for me. I think that most intellectually honest Christians are going to need a little more clarity.

These ancient laws may seem a bit absurd or extreme; however, our modern-day legal system is littered with strange laws, most of which are from the last one hundred years.

Did you know it's illegal in Fairbanks, Alaska, to feed alcoholic beverages to a moose? How many drunken moose altercations did it take before someone put their foot down? Or did you know it's illegal in San Francisco to wipe your car with used underwear. (Personally, that makes sense to me.) But I've always wondered how the police would determine if it's used or not, legally speaking. In South Bend, Indiana, it's illegal for monkeys to smoke cigarettes, a law that I'd still support today. Or in Pennsylvania, ministers are forbidden from performing marriages when either the bride or groom is drunk, which makes sense. But such a law in Wisconsin, where I grew up, would have nullified 90 percent of all weddings.

Every culture has its share of excesses, right? No one wants to live around inebriated moose or chain-smoking monkeys. Thus, our laws can become a rather strange necessity. The Civil/Political Laws of the Old Testament are no exception.

The last set of laws in the Old Testament are Ceremonial Laws, which were regulations that governed the worship rituals of God's people. These are the parts of the Old Testament that the book of Hebrews and Colossians refer to as fulfilled. Christ became our Passover lamb (1 Cor. 5:6–8). Christ became our high priest, our sacrifice, once for all time (Heb. 5:5; 7:27; 9:12). And His work on the cross is the ultimate fulfillment of the Sabbath. Thus, Paul and other Bible authors argued these rituals and laws were nothing more than a shadow of things to come (Col. 2:16–17; Heb. 9:10; 10:1). They were an object lesson—an analogy of sorts—pointing to a greater reality fulfilled in Christ (Heb. 9:23–24).

We would still be smart to obey the Moral Law. Disciplines like tithing, not stealing, or not committing adultery are no less relevant (and perhaps ignored) today than they were in Bible times. These principles generally predated the Mosaic Law and spoke to transcendent human sin problems, things like selfishness, lust, or not putting God first.

However, some Christians falsely assume that everything from the Old Testament is suddenly obsolete with the New Testament. And, yes, that might be true of the ceremonial facets of the Law. But if we love people, we still need to tell them when the stove is hot (i.e., teach the Moral Law).

This doesn't mean we should do this by being judgmental idiots. But that's why Paul said we must be careful to use the Law in context. Simply put, the Moral Law (aka truth) is like a butter knife: You can use it to make sandwiches for the neighbor kids or you can kill them with it. Paul also said, "He has made us competent as ministers of a new covenant—not of the letter but of the Spirit; for the letter kills, but the Spirit gives life" (2 Cor. 3:6).

The difference between a Pharisee and a Christian is not that one teaches the Law and the other doesn't. Rather, the difference is in how the Law is taught and the motives that drive our obedience to the Law. There are entire ministries designed around obnoxious people telling others about the Moral Law minus any kindness that might actually lead to repentance.

Many Christians falsely think that through logic and persuasive words they can lead people to biblical repentance. And, yes, we can motivate people to do all sorts of things through logic, guilt, or other influence techniques. But if a person's repentance isn't a true response to God's kindness, then we need to seriously question whether such a repentance is a biblical one.

To put this another way: Many Christians falsely think that evangelism is the proclamation of truth. But the Bible teaches that it's truth plus a relationship with the Spirit of life (Rom. 8). In fact, the apostle Paul taught that ministering truth by itself is propagating the law of sin and death (Rom. 7). It's worse than giving medicine without the spoonful of sugar; it's indigestible. Thus, when sinners get angry at our incomplete gospel proclamations, many legalistic Christians think they're being persecuted. But, in reality, their victims are nothing more than little kids vomiting up their ill-advised approach to medicine.

At my church, we've come to term these practices as *spiritual abortions*. Every human being has a spiritual gestation period. And without kindness or a loving community, they have no ability to be born again in the biblical sense. Despite these biblical prerequisites, many Christians can't stand being a patient witness of God's kindness. The end result is the use of unhealthy tactics that prematurely deliver spiritual babies before they're ready.

When we take these shortcuts to influencing people, it's a lot like

Despite these biblical prerequisites, many Christians can't stand being a patient witness of God's kindness. The end result is the use of unhealthy tactics that prematurely deliver spiritual babies before they're ready.

jamming big chunks of meat down a baby's throat and then wondering why the baby dies. We can pretend that people have rejected our meaty gospel. What they're rejecting is our pharisaical approaches to transformation. And deep in their hearts, people know when they are encountering divine kindness versus human religiosity.

IDENTIFYING A COUNTERFEIT

It's similar to how my five-year-old son recently responded at a grade school band concert. The emcee finished an elaborate description of the first song. But the moment the fifth-grade band started playing, it sounded like a bunch of offbeat clangs and clunks. To my astonishment, my son stood up on his seat and yelled with a betrayed look on his face, "Wait! That's not music!" as if something was being deviously foisted upon a crowd of innocent listeners. I immediately tried to put my hand over his mouth. But, like William Wallace in *Braveheart*, he passionately repeated it, each time with more resolve.

As my hand clasped over his confused face, the whole crowd snickered at his adorable honesty. We all pretended that it wasn't true. He looked at me as though I was an accessory to a crime. Like most children, they call things as they see them. And quite often, they're right.

Likewise, we've all had false religion forced upon us. And when our childlike faith challenged the disparity, much like my son, many of us had the voices of religious adulthood cover our mouths. As a result, we ingested a gospel that was devoid of good news. In some ways, this entire book is dedicated to my son's honest and pure impulse.

Let's not become lost in the silly things that Pharisees do. In upcoming chapters, we'll make sure to devote a good amount of time to those diseases. So instead, let's see if we might have a sneaky Pharisee of our own lurking inside. As I introduce the following two approaches to the Law, ask yourself this question: Which of these approaches do I tend to embrace most often?

The Legalistic Approach to God's Law

The pharisaical approach is the epitome of legalism. It occurs when we obey God's Moral Law to earn God's love and attain God's righteousness. Key symptoms may include:

- Striving
- A lack of the fruit of the Holy Spirit (Gal. 5:22–23)
- A consistent lack of motivation for things like prayer or Bible reading
- Quite often, the commands of God feel like a curse
- Obedience feels hard
- God routinely feels distant or perhaps disinterested

The Grace-Driven Approach to God's Law

On the other hand, we have the grace-driven approach. This occurs when we understand God's free gift of grace. Shockingly, our righteousness has nothing to do with our behavior. God scandalously applies righteousness to our sin-drenched souls out of pure generosity. Key symptoms may include:

- Feeling like you just won the lottery
- A desire to shout and scream like a crazy person
- A strong desire to meet with this God over and over in prayer

In a grace-driven approach, we don't obey because we have to but because we want to. The Moral Law, which condemned us outside of Christ, has now become our worship list. Obedience is now just one of the fun ways we say thanks to Him while He drenches us with favor; it naturally flows from our lives. Christianity is not a process

> *Shockingly, our righteousness has nothing to do with our behavior. God scandalously applies righteousness to our sin-drenched souls out of pure generosity.*

in which we earn love; it's a process in which we reflect love. Or as it's often said, "We are not saved *by* good works. We're saved *for* good works!"

For the Christian, the Bible isn't a list of requirements but a list of results after experiencing God's love. Righteousness is not the reward of living rightly. It's the unmerited gift that, once understood, irresistibly results in right living. And suddenly the motivating energy that drives our quest for morality changes from striving to being thankful for what God has already done in and through us. This has a profound effect on how joy-filled and grateful your faith becomes and has a dramatic affect on how you motivate those around you to serve the Lord.

So which of these two approaches do you live out more? If you're like me, you probably vacillate between the two of them quite often. So the real questions become: How do we stop this craziness? How do we tip ourselves into the grace-driven approach once and for all?

Truth be told, it's incredibly easy to pick up burdens that God never called us to carry (Matt. 11:28). Even more, there's still a part of us that wants to earn God's righteousness. And why? Grace just doesn't seem fair! And, honestly, it's not fair. But you're lying to yourself if you think you can start earning His love. So allow me to give you a better analogy of who you are in Christ. I hope this will thoroughly persuade you to abandon all of your legalistic pursuits once and for all.

YOU ARE A DOORKNOB

I've always liked celebrity auctions because they reveal how silly we all are. Some famous person blows their nose, and the rest of us immediately start bidding on the tissue. Then we can brag about our majestically framed snot-rag (and how it reveals our tight bond with the blower) when our friends come over. Our secret hope is that it will make them want to be our friends even more. (At least that's how it worked for me in fifth grade when I got my favorite professional wrestler's autograph.)

A while ago the news reported that someone spent a fanatical amount of money purchasing a creaky old doorknob from the estate sale of Marilyn Monroe. It was mind-blowing what this stupid old doorknob sold for. Of course it wasn't even a high-quality doorknob, not that I'm a doorknob expert. But I certainly know it had no intrinsic value except for the fact that it belonged to Marilyn Monroe.

It's the same way for those of us who belong to Christ. On our own, we're just another doorknob. What makes us special is that Jesus touched us. Just as the doorknob in the auction had gained merit by being associated with Marilyn Monroe, our merit comes from being associated with Christ. Now you might still be tempted to say, "But God: Look at me! I'm a freaking great doorknob! I read my Bible more than others. I even return rogue shopping carts in the grocery store parking lot." May I lovingly remind you that you're still an old doorknob.

Your righteousness, worthiness, and ability to qualify for God's favor is not based on any intrinsic worth (Titus 3:5). Sadly, you—even on your greatest day—*still* fall short of God's glory (Rom. 3:23), which is why our value is entirely based upon whom we belong to—Christ.

Whether they admit it or not, every church still struggles with the legalistic tendency to set up new ways to earn God's love. Many churches teach tithing or unknown tongues as though they were an obligation or sign of elitism rather than a celebration. Indeed, you can turn just about any command of God into an obligation.

Many Christians even turn their worship formats into an indispensible means for earning God's favor as though God is suddenly impressed that we cried 4.5 extra tears and did a full fifteen more minutes of [fill in the blank] than the church down the road. And suddenly God is so impressed that He exclaims, "Wow! Take a look at that doorknob! I haven't even touched it, yet it's gotta be worth thousands. Wow! I better visit that church." It sounds absurd because it is absurd.

I bring this up to remind us that we're really no different than the Pharisees most of the time. They depended upon their purity rituals as the notch in their belts that made them feel special. No one wants to admit they're just a doorknob who has been touched by someone special. Jesus doesn't estimate spiritual value the same way we do.

We can look at first-century Pharisees as though they were freaky-weird; but, sometimes the only way we're different is that we spiritualize a different set of rituals or values. In the end, none of us will gain access to heaven because we worshiped God for His favorite length of time or had the perfect amount of great theology.

Truth be told, we all are going to look back on our imperfect worship and theology and cringe at some point in this life and the life to come. We're going to cry, "Oh God! I can't even believe you took any pleasure in our ridiculous attempts to praise you." And God will say, "That's because I took pleasure in the Christ that is in you, your hope of glory, not your formats or your lame attempts at theological perfection."

So here's a question for you: What degree of perfect theology and methodology does God require before He allows you into heaven? If we understand the Scriptures, this very question is a sign that we've missed the point. "For it is by grace you have been saved, through faith—and this not from yourselves, it is the gift of God—not by works, so that no one can boast" (Eph. 2:8–9). This includes tithing, tongues, expository sermons, and perfect theology. Paul continued in Colossians when he said, "See to it that no one takes you captive through hollow and deceptive philosophy." He understood that all our earthly attempts to please God outside of grace "[depend] on human tradition and the elemental spiritual forces of this world rather than on Christ" (Col. 2:8).

In Christ, faith is our only obligation; the rest of God's Law is celebration. I still wouldn't recommend killing your neighbors or ignoring tithes, tongues, or any other spiritual opportunities. Indeed, we'd be fools to ignore basic morality or to avoid experiencing these powerful gifts. But let's not turn tools or gifts into obligations. Although the difference is small, it's profound. And like my son at that concert, we should stand and confront the disparity as small as it might seem.

Here's the real reason why my son confronted the band that day: He loves music. And his five-year-old heart isn't afraid to bust a move when the music is right. But what happens if the world around him fails to see the disparity? He just might have to spend the rest of his life tolerating an empty counterfeit. And many of you have done that long enough with Christianity. Stand up for God's sake! Abandon all pretenses of value, and the Christ in you will bring you to an overwhelming glory so great that an eternity of praise could never and should never satisfy you.

CHAPTER TWO IN REVIEW

Key Ideas

1. There are three types of Law in the Old Testament: Moral, Civil/Political, and Ceremonial.

2. There are no shortcuts to spiritual formation.

3. The difference between a Pharisee and a Christian is how the Law is taught and the motives that drive such obedience.

4. Real evangelism is the "proclamation of truth" plus a relationship with the Spirit of life.

5. The legalistic approach to God's Law occurs when we obey God's Moral Law so as to earn God's love and attain His righteousness.

6. The grace-driven approach to God's Law occurs when we understand God's free gift of grace.

7. Obedience is one of the fun ways we say thanks to Him while He drenches us with favor; yet, it naturally flows from our lives.

8. For the Christian, the Bible isn't a list of requirements but a list of results after experiencing God's love.

9. Righteousness is not the reward of living rightly; it's the unmerited gift that irresistibly results in right living.

10. "Christ in you" brings an overwhelming glory so great that an eternity of praise could never and should never satisfy you.

Discussion Questions

1. Have you ever struggled to understand the Old Testament Law? How did the "three types of Law" proposed in this chapter bring clarity or confusion to your understanding of Old Testament rules?

2. Which approach to God's Law—legalistic or grace-driven—most often motivates you?

3. What is the danger of living with a legalistic approach to God's Law?

4. If kindness is what truly leads people to repentance, how might this change the way we share the gospel?

5. In your opinion, what are some examples of people taking short-cuts to sharing the gospel?

6. Is there anyone you'd like to share the gospel with? What are some practical ways that you could show them the kindness of God?

7. Looking at your spiritual history, has your tendency been to fall into the grace-driven approach or the legalistic approach? Do you feel you're still striving a lot when it comes to your relationship with God? What causes you to say this?

8. Why do you suppose we like to earn righteousness? What is it that causes us to want to perform for God? How does this compare to how God imparts righteousness?

9. On a scale of 1 to 10 (with 10 being absolute right living), how would you rate your right living? What does your rating say about your understanding of God's grace?

10. Describe a time when you were bored with worship. What would you change about that experience if you could go back in time?

CHAPTER THREE

The Art of Giving Your All

How do we get radical without being religious?

Dɪᴅ ʏᴏᴜ ᴋɴᴏᴡ ᴛʜᴀᴛ ғʀᴇQᴜᴇɴᴛ ᴄʜᴜʀᴄʜ attendance dramatically increases your life expectancy? In fact, epidemiologists (doctors who study epidemics) have routinely documented a striking difference and significant health improvement for those who devoutly participate in God-centered social groups versus those who don't.[7] Another study found that church attendance dramatically increases your odds of sexual satisfaction.[8] (I promise I'm not making this up, and I promise that stat will grow your church.) In fact, that same study found that people who attend church *twice* a week even have greater . . . well, you get the idea. There are certainly a lot of benefits to serving God. And whenever I share these benefits, church attendance gets a little bit easier for everyone.

I could take a slightly more pharisaical approach and simply threaten people, "You might make God mad!" or "You might lose your salvation if you don't come to church." As many pastors try to do, I could shame people into coming to church. But why give guilt trips when Scripture give us endless positive incentives for obedience?

Remember, the kingdom of heaven is a treasure, not an obligation. In fact, I would go as far as to say if obedience to any command from God's Word is joyless for you—even radical obedience—then you probably aren't experiencing the power of biblical obedience.

Don't misunderstand me. Christianity is all about carrying crosses. God has a call on all of our lives, and sometimes that call can get painful. But even Christ endured His cross "for the joy set before him" (Heb. 12:2). Jesus had such a beautifully intoxicating vision of the future that the present cost was easily worth it. As I mentioned before, Christians often preach the suffering of the cross *minus* the joy set before us. Thus, Scripture becomes a tool that oppresses people more than uplifts them. It is supposed to be good news.

Recently, God called me to make a radical sacrifice. And I have to admit, the task that God challenged me with took my breath away. His challenge confronted the very foundations of my faith. But before I tell you what happened, it's important you understand the backstory.

At Substance, we're constantly launching new portable campuses and spiritual hospitals all over the city in order to accommodate growth. Yet based on our demographics, it's incredibly rare to meet a person who's even heard the word *tithing*[9] before, let alone people who dare to actually do it.

I often get a little jealous when I hear some of my southern pastor friends talk about their church incomes. It almost seems as though half of their members came out of the womb tithing. When our church broke two thousand attendees, we were lucky if even eighty people gave anything. Obviously, part of this is due to the youthfulness of our church. Yet, even still, it makes ministry and facility planning in a fast-growing, barely churched congregation like ours a complicated task.

Recently, my wife and I were hoping to upgrade our house. We live in a small 1950s-style ranch house in an economically depressed part of the city. For a megachurch pastor, people are often startled by how conservatively we live. All five of our family members share a singular, small bathroom sink (and

> *Jesus had such a beautifully intoxicating vision of the future that the present cost was easily worth it.*

three of the five are women). For the last five years, we've been saving up a large down payment with the hopes of an upgrade. Yet, as we planned to launch our fourth church campus, we also felt God was personally asking us to make additional financial sacrifices.

My wife and I have always given away 15 percent of our income as a starting point. We've given away as much as 50 percent. And this is partly because we've always felt that contentment and financial generosity are the heartbeat of the gospel, not to mention a great way to move the heart of God (Prov. 11:25; Acts 10:4).

Did you know that if you're combined household income exceeds $40,000, then you are in the top 3 percent of the world's wealthiest people?[10] When we talk about great wealth, we often focus on the fortunes of people like Bill Gates or Mark Zuckerberg—the .000,000,01 percent rich—when in reality most of us are mega-rich compared to the rest of the world. And since my income exceeds this 3 percent, I find it irresistibly fun to sow my money into kingdom causes. None of our previous acts of generosity, however, compared to the request that God was about to ask of us.

DID I HEAR YOU RIGHT?

As I was praying about the amount God wanted us to sacrifice for this new campus launch, I finally asked my wife, "Of all the accounts that we can touch, how much do we even have?" My wife (who's a great bean counter) started outlining all of our accounts: "We've got $23,000 in our emergency fund, $9,000 in our automotive mutual fund . . ." And she continued listing off all of our investments and bank accounts. I had to admit I was a bit impressed by how much my wife and I had saved up. Suddenly, as she listed off our last five years of savings, I felt the Holy Spirit impress upon my heart, "Peter, I want you to give it ALL away."

Immediately I thought, "That CAN'T be the Lord! I rebuke that thought!" Perhaps it was my overactive imagination. After all, sometimes it's easy to mistake our own thoughts for God's thoughts, right? Or perhaps I was hearing him incorrectly? I mean, maybe

God was saying, "I want you to go to the MALL, not I want you to give it ALL." Or what if it was the devil trying to trick me?

As my heart was racing, I stopped for a second and thought, "Why would the devil want me to give more money to the gospel?"

This fear of radical obedience is an experience that every single one of us will struggle with at some point or another.

But I kept trying to think of reasons why this was silliness. I mean, how am I going to sell this to my wife? How will I tell my financial advisor? He's going to think we're crazy, perhaps suicidal. What about the new house we've been dreaming about for years? Our kids are sick and tired of bunking together. Can I really tolerate our tiny square footage any longer? It would take years before we could upgrade, let alone get our financial margin back.

The truth was I did hear the Lord correctly. God has never forsaken us before. So the real question was, why was I suddenly so scared to obey? And before I share the rest of this story, I think this is a profound question to stop and meditate on. This fear of radical obedience is an experience that every single one of us will struggle with at some point or another. So how do we deal with these fears, and what is actually lurking behind these feelings?

FIRE IN THE FIREPLACE

I vividly remember having this same feeling as a new believer. I came upon numerous Bible texts that call us to avoid sexual activity outside of marriage. To be honest, my first response was, "No way! Who in their right mind would obey that?" I actually remember saying to God, "Prove it." I'm kind of an analytical skeptic, especially when I'm required to change something. And, as if on cue, the next several days I kept running into a jaw-dropping number of secular university studies on sex.

To my shock and surprise, it's a statistical fact that those who have sex outside of marriage are more likely to:

- break up or get divorced,[11]
- experience physical abuse (odds double),[12]
- experience emotional abuse,[13]
- experience anxiety and depression,[14]
- be sexually dissatisfied,[15]
- feel guilt and ongoing sexual inhibition,[16] and
- commit adultery in the future.[17]

And this was just the beginning of the research. They kept jumping out at me wherever I looked.

When I read all of this research, I started feeling angry at our American culture. I felt as though I had been lied to about my sexuality. I was a bit surprised by the sheer enormity of information that I had either completely missed or ignored. That entire week I felt as if God kept heckling me with a smile, "You wanted proof, right?"

Obedience to God's Word regarding sexual purity suddenly became a lot easier after doing my research. Notice I didn't say easy, but easier. But who in their right mind wants to have increased depression, anxiety, adultery, and divorce rates? I suppose obedience became easier because I realized that the God who created my sexuality has my best interests in mind. What if the very same God who created my sexuality is actually a good God, a God who has an amazing plan for me? What if He's not a killjoy? Once I finally accepted a biblical revelation of who He really was, obedience was actually fun. I started to understand what the Bible calls an obedience that *comes from faith*. And remember that phrase because, as you're about to see, it's incredibly important.

For example, in Romans 1:5–6, the apostle Paul explains that we have a unique message—a message that sets us apart from other preachers who peddle oppressive religion: "Through [Christ] and for his name's sake, we received grace and apostleship to call people from among all the Gentiles to the obedience that comes from faith."

Notice that Paul isn't talking about obedience that comes from obligation, shame, or fear. Certainly, these three tools can be a powerful form of motivation. I hate to admit it, but sometimes it seems as though half of the books in Christian bookstores are designed around this approach. But Paul intentionally distanced himself from these inferior motivators because he knew they would ultimately lead to failure.

Christians aren't called only to proclaim truth. We're called to inspire faith, grounded in truth, out of which obedience naturally flows. As in the above example about sexuality, God gave me a few reasons to keep fire in the fireplace. He didn't yell at me. He didn't shame me or make my desires out to be dirty. Rather, He kindly gave me a few secular confirmations to propel me into a biblical lifestyle. That is to say, He got into my world, as silly as that world was. And once His subtle strategy to subvert my views took root, obedience naturally started flowing. Most important, it was joyful!

Many churches simply shame people into action. They often quote Scripture in which Jesus offended the masses. And yes, there are parts of the gospel that are unavoidably difficult. Yet this narrow stereotype of the "Offensive Jesus" simply doesn't jive with the greater teachings of Christ where sinners constantly ran *to* Him. Most of His offensive teachings were directed toward the religiously diseased. He'd literally measure back to them the same oppressive measures they were using (Matt. 7:2).

But these oppressive approaches to radical Christianity are silly for two reasons. First of all, sin has built-in consequences all by itself. If you are hell-bent on touching a hot stove . . . fine. Let's see how it works out for you. You don't have to take my word for it. Besides, the school of hard knocks has an incredibly effective curriculum.

> *Christians aren't called only to proclaim truth. We're called to inspire faith, grounded in truth, out of which obedience naturally flows.*

Further, if I highjack the role of the Holy Spirit in your life (John 16:8), you'll probably sever your relationship with me. Sinning is a lot like eating chocolate-covered poop. If you're convinced that you're missing out, despite my constant warnings, I refuse to manipulate you. When you become aware that the warm morsel of filth in your mouth was less than satisfying, you're going to need a friend nearby. And I want to be that friend standing with a big bowl of spiritual ice cream or at least some mouthwash. (I'll let you choose.)

How would you ever find your way to my bowl of ice cream if I motivated you with shame? If I shame you with oppressive teachings or repeatedly make you feel like an idiot (to motivate you), chances are you would reject our relationship (and your refreshing bowl of ice cream). This, unfortunately, is a good picture of how dead religion has previously worked in many of our lives.

Quite often we heard the truth, but it wasn't life-giving truth. We heard the call for obedience, but it wasn't an obedience built upon freshly inspired faith (Rom.1:5–6). Thus, even if it motivated us for a season, we finally decided that we weren't any happier living under constant condemnation. Hence, we decided to go back and take another bite of chocolate-covered poop. At least *that* was sweet for a moment.

Paul argues in Romans 1:5 that we aren't merely calling people to obedience; rather, we're calling people to an obedience that results from our faith. To preach truth without inspiring faith is a false gospel. It has little power to bring about sustained change. And even if we succeed in creating some mutant form of obedience, it will hardly feel joyful, let alone glorify God. That's why my primary goal as a teacher of the gospel isn't to proclaim truth. It's to isolate unbelief and inspire faith.[18]

What are the hardest commands for you to keep? What are the habits you want to start or stop? I always begin with the question: What is this sin my answer to? Or, what is the legitimate God-given need in me that I'm filling with inferior substitutes? You see, in all of these things, you might think you have an obedience problem when you actually have a faith problem. You might be able to motivate yourself with shame for short time, giving yourself a semblance of progress, but if you don't deal with the root cause—your lack of faith—you'll just be going down the path of dead religion.

So if obedience naturally flows from faith, how do we keep our faith stirred up? Faith is like leaky fuel, especially when we're going through a crisis. So allow me to give you two powerful tools that will keep your faith-tank full: *constant meditation* and *inconveniently godly friends*.

CONSTANT MEDITATION

I love the story where the disciples were trying to cast out a demon but weren't able to. As a result, the disciples were having a squabble with the teachers of the Law. Jesus, just coming off a prayer retreat, walks onto the scene and immediately casts the demon out. A bit confused, the disciples asked Jesus why He was able to do it while they, on the other hand, looked like impotent dorks. Christ's reply is quite profound, "This kind can come out only by prayer" (Mark 9:29). If you want authority over tough spiritual situations, like this demon, you've got to live a lifestyle of prayer. Theological squabbling is a common by-product of spiritual impotence, but this isn't the only passage that shows miraculous favor upon those who pray more often.

Daniel, an important Old Testament character, was a man of prayer and fasting. An angel even told him, "As soon as you began to pray, an answer was given, which I have come to tell you, for you are highly esteemed" (Dan. 9:23). The Bible certainly isn't implying that God loves certain people more than others; however, the Bible is clear that everyone does not get the same results. So, once again, we could infer that there is a connection between prayer and miracles in Scripture.

In fact, right now there are many of you with problems that you feel unable to conquer. Like the disciples, you've invoked all the right formulas from Scripture; yet,

> *Theological squabbling is a common by-product of spiritual impotence.*

your problem still seems to flop around and scream at you. I don't want to oversimplify things, but what if, like the disciples, your life-style of prayer and fasting has something to be desired? And if that's the case, it's time to employ meditation.

One of the most powerful types of prayer is meditation. Most people think of prayer as asking God for things (aka supplication), but Jesus taught that too much supplication is a sign of dysfunction (Matt. 6:7–8). Healthy prayer, however, requires listening to God as well; and, one of the greatest ways God speaks is through His Word. That's why if we want to get to know God, we've got to spend a sub-stantial amount of time memorizing, meditating, and praying His Word (Josh. 1:8; Ps. 1). Not surprisingly, when Jesus prayed and fasted, He said, "Man shall not live on bread alone, but on every word that comes from the mouth of God" (Matt. 4:4). Listening to God is foundational.

If you don't know what meditation is, let me explain. Meditation is basically thinking deeply on every word in the promises of God. It's literally the process of dwelling upon each and every word. In fact, a good sermon is essentially a corporate meditation on a specific Scripture verse or passage. And when you get good at meditating, a rather profound process ensues.

For every problem we could have, God has a promise to answer it. But knowing God's Word isn't enough—believing that it is true is what counts. And that is exactly what meditation does. Meditation is the process of converting truth into spiritual fuel. It turns head knowledge into heart knowledge. Or, as Hebrews 4:2 puts it, God's word must be "combined with faith" before it will achieve its super-natural results.

Recently a friend of mine was going through a rough spot finan-cially. He tithed regularly, but one week was particularly rough. He calculated his tithe to be $350, yet he wanted every dollar to stay in his savings. So he wrestled through it by asking, "Should I give it to the church? Should I hold onto it?"

At church that morning I happened to be teaching on Prov-erbs 3:9–10, which says, "Honor the LORD with your wealth, with the firstfruits of all your crops; then your barns will be filled to overflowing, and your vats will brim over with new wine." I was reminding the church that there's an incredible cause and effect that God is daring

> *Prayer-filled meditation is what causes us to stay faithful while the miraculous is incubating.*

us to participate in. In many ways, we were corporately meditating on this Scripture. And, like a lot of people, my friend felt faith rise in his heart.

He decided to write out his tithe check for $350. And get this, that very month he brought in the largest commission he had ever gotten, almost exactly one hundred times his tithe check! Do the math. That's a lot of money to make in one month. In fact, he set a new company record for the biggest week ever. But even more amazing, none of these sales leads had been in his pipeline. They came straight out of nowhere. You can't tell me that's a coincidence.

Prayer-filled meditation is what causes us to stay faithful while the miraculous is incubating. Thus, even if we lack the authority of Daniel or Jesus, Christ still assures us that we can be delivered when we are faithful and obedient in prayer and fasting.

INCONVENIENTLY GODLY FRIENDSHIPS

The second incubator of faith (and thus, obedience) is a bit more practical: Find godly friends. And by *godly friends* I don't mean religious friends (aka people who motivate themselves with obligation, shame, or fear). I love this quote I've heard from many different sources: "Show me your friends, and I'll show you your future." The Bible is constantly calling us to be cautious about our relationships (Prov. 12:26; 13:20; 2 Cor. 6:14; 1 Cor. 15:33; Heb. 10:24–25).

Many studies have found that one of the single greatest statistical predictors of spiritual growth is having a high quantity of intimate Christian friends.[19] Not surprisingly, it's also one of the largest statistical predictors of church health, church growth, as well as church satisfaction.[20] Naturally, research like this has altered the way I think about church. And, keep in mind, your friends affect far more than just your spirituality.

Constant meditation and inconveniently godly friends have a profound effect on our ability to obey and enjoy God.

Did you know that having supportive friends doubles your odds of surviving cancer,[21] stroke,[22] and heart disease?[23] Scientific research now shows we can significantly predict happiness, stress, memory loss,[24] weight,[25] life expectancy, and odds of quitting smoking[26] exclusively based on your quantity and quality of friends!

In fact, research is now discovering that even our genetic code can be affected by those we hang around![27] So, most certainly, our friends will affect every aspect of our faith. Quite simply, our fellowship is the single most important aspect of our physical spiritual and emotional well-being. Suddenly, our criteria for choosing jobs, churches, and even spouses dramatically changes.

So it's critical that we surround ourselves with people who inconveniently and outwardly pursue their faith. We need friends like Stephen of Acts 6:5, who was chosen because he was "a man full of faith and of the Holy Spirit."

Which of your friends stir up your faith in a life-giving way? And what are you going to do to get around them more? Constant meditation and inconveniently godly friends have a profound effect on our ability to obey and enjoy God.

GIVING MY ALL

Coming back to my story, I was so scared to empty all my investments and bank accounts for Christ. But I immediately started bringing Scripture promises to mind. I started meditating on Scripture promises like Proverbs 11:25, "A generous person will prosper; whoever refreshes others will be refreshed." And "Whoever sows sparingly will also reap sparingly, and whoever sows generously will also reap generously" (2 Cor. 9:6). Before long, I started getting this giddy feeling that I may have stumbled upon the greatest investment opportunity on earth. It wasn't oppressive; it was joyful. But what would my wife think?

Right when I was about to tell her my thoughts she blurted, "I think we should give it all!" Immediately, we glared at each other with wide-eyed grins. "Really?" I grimaced. It was a total rush, perhaps a holy moment. When we both finally breathed, we started thinking about the logistics of it all: How do we involve our kids in this decision? How do we tell our financial advisor? And, what might this affect in our immediate future, things like family vacations?

Truth be told, it took a lot of work to give away all that money. And there was still a grieving process that we had to go through. Even to this day, every time I see a beautiful house, I ache a little. Every time my daughters leave their hair dryers on our small bathroom sink, I moan. I hate living in a neighborhood where cars get jacked all the time. And it kills my wife that we have a terrible house for hosting people. Yet there's always going to be something to whine about. There's always going to be something to tempt us to say, "God, I'll be generous next year."

Honestly, it's the little things that make generosity hard. For example, I'd been looking at snow blowers for the previous two years. When you live in a place that can get over eight feet of snow in the winter, there are some things that become a necessity. Yet every dollar needed to go right back into our emergency fund. So the last thing I could afford was a snow blower.

No matter where I went, there seemed to be these gorgeous snow blowers for sale. Like an alcoholic walking through a bar, it seemed as if the devil was torturing me. One day, as I was walking through a home improvement store, I saw the shiniest, reddest snow blower I've ever seen. It was almost as though heaven was shining down on it. So,

> *There's always going to be something to whine about. There's always going to be something to tempt us to say, "God, I'll be generous next year."*

at last, I broke down and started ranting at God, "God, this is torture! I'm trying to put you first financially, but Lord, are you even in this? Did I make a foolish decision?"

Later that day, I was visiting a church to hear a guest speaker. And even while worship was going on, I found myself continuing to rant at God, "I was foolish to give all our money away!" And, no lie, the minister, who I didn't even know, literally called me out of the audience and said, "The Lord just spoke to me about you and told me to tell you that you have answered God's call to produce wealth." I was a bit shocked. He continued, "And because you have answered God's call, He will open up doors of significance for you."

I don't know about you, but I'm not sure that God could get any clearer than this. My wife and I were literally buzzing for the rest of the night. As we went home, snow blowers were the last thing on my mind. If God can supernaturally speak to us through a total stranger, then He can certainly take care of our practical needs.

Then suddenly, we got a phone call from this delightful couple in our church. Shockingly, they said, "At our last worship night, God told us to buy you guys a brand new snow blower. And, we were wondering . . . when can we drop it off?"

Keep in mind, I never told anyone about this need. So, what are the odds? God's not kidding around when He promises that if you'll put His kingdom first, He'll add things into your life (Matt. 6:33).

And guess what? That winter brought one of the highest quantities of snow in Minnesota history (over eight feet). Every time that snow blower growled to a start, I felt like having a Pentecostal worship service. Even crazier than God providing that snow blower, the moment my wife and I secretly made that decision, our weekly church income suddenly jumped by over 35 percent, and stayed that high. That's a huge amount of money. It's hard for me to see all of these things as a coincidence.

Obedience isn't always easy; but, it's always joyful. My personal wealth hasn't necessarily bounced back yet. But my fulfillment is at a record high, along with my trust in God. That's why I never try to be faithful to God. Instead, I try to be full of faith, and faithfulness naturally results. You may call it semantics, but I call it a Pharisectomy. And as my large pile of personal miracle stories stack up, so does my faith in the One who is faithful.

We don't need shame, guilt, or obligation to motivate us. And even when people foolishly touch the hot stove, we needn't give them lectures or I-told-you-so's. We give them modern-day miracle stories, the details of which are so specific that it leaves them wondering: What if God really does care about me? Well, guess what? He does care about you! And when this kind of faith grips your heart, prepare for an irresistible obedience—even radical obedience—that will turn your world head-over-heels.

CHAPTER THREE IN REVIEW

Key Ideas

1. The kingdom of heaven is a treasure, not an obligation.

2. Fear of radical obedience is an experience that every single one of us will struggle with at some point or another.

3. Christians aren't called to proclaim truth; we're called to inspire faith in the truth.

4. Most of Jesus' offensive teachings were directed toward the religiously diseased.

5. To preach truth without inspiring people's faith is a false gospel.

6. There are two powerful tools that will keep your faith-tank full: constant meditation and inconveniently godly friends.

7. Theological squabbling is a common by-product of spiritual impotence.

8. Prayer-filled meditation is what causes us to stay faithful while the miraculous is incubating.

9. It's critical that we surround ourselves with people who inconveniently and outwardly pursue their faith.

10. Obedience isn't always easy, but it's always joyful.

Discussion Questions

1. Have you ever felt oppressed with truth instead of uplifted by it? What do you think are the differences? Can you think of any examples?

2. Authentic Christianity is all about carrying crosses. What does *carrying crosses* mean to you? Are you carrying crosses? Explain your response.

3. What are some ways you can inspire faith in the truth? What is the difference between this and proclaiming the truth?

4. What are three ways you can meditate on God's Word? What did God teach you the last time you meditated on His Word?

5. You will become like the people with whom you associate. If this is true, where is your life headed? Are you satisfied with this image of your future? Why or why not?

6. If you're comfortable sharing: Are there any areas in which you've experienced a fear of obeying? What were they? Why do you think you felt that way?

7. Have you ever meditated on Scripture before? If so, do you have any suggestions about when, how, or where to do it?

8. In light of the influence of friends on our lives, how does this change the way you think about your job, your church, and your family?

9. If a person lacks friends or has less than healthy friends, how might they change them? How might our job, commute, or families affect our ability to change friends?

10. How have others tried to play the role of the Holy Spirit in your life? What was the end result of these situations?

CHAPTER FOUR

Checkbook Christianity

Why did sinners run to Christ even though His messages were tough?

Every church has that one person who takes too much responsibility for the spiritual and theological hygiene of everyone else. I call them *church rebukers*. They're not always easy to recognize because they don't all grow long beards and carry stone tablets anymore. You see, church rebukers come in all shapes and sizes.

I'll never forget the first time a woman stood up in the middle of my message and started screaming at me. (Believe it or not, I've had three over the years.) I'm sure there were probably a few messages where I actually deserved such a crazy person, but that specific message was quite tame. The Lord knows I was being a good little boy (e.g., no swear words).

But most church rebukers use more subtle approaches. In charismatic churches, you'll experience something that I call *prophelying*. People share their silly opinion and then say, "God told me to say this to you."

One time I finished preaching and two people lined up to talk. The first said, "That message was terrible! The Spirit has been irreparably grieved." And, no lie, the very next person said, "That message moved the heart of God! He is totally pleased with you." You see, either the Holy Spirit needs to take an anti-depressant, or people are prophelying.

But church leaders aren't the only people who get targeted. It's easy for any long-term member of the body of Christ to get cynical about God's people over time. After experiencing phenomena like these for years, I've had to create a special list of truly spiritual people who are uniquely qualified to get in my face. Otherwise, I would have either quit being teachable or simply quit being a leader entirely.

Another clever technique church rebukers use is called *accusigizing*. They accuse people, but it's couched in an apology. They usually approach you with a sappy look in their eyes saying, "Hey, I just wanted to apologize to you . . . you see, I've been nursing a grudge, telling all my friends about how you manipulate people. But, I'm sorry 'bout that." Thus, they compel you to fish out their piranha with your bare hands.

A similar technique is what I call the *confrontation-affirmation*. You sneak a confrontation into an encouragement, "You wanna know what I love about you? Some people get all concerned about wearing stylish clothing or personal hygiene; but, you . . . you're free . . . I *love* that!"

Being a die-hard songwriter, I've always enjoyed being in various worship bands. Early on, I remember being in a band with a guy named Billy. He was a vocalist who, bless his heart, couldn't sing to save his life. (A good Christian always blesses someone's heart before ripping him to shreds. It somehow nullifies the bad things we're about to say.) And right before our team leader removed Billy from the team, he started out with a classic confrontation-affirmation line, "Billy, you know what I like about you . . ." We all perked up with wide eyes. We knew what was coming. "Billy, you have a worshiper's heart. Some people get all focused on singing in tune, but you . . . you just focus on God." Of course, when a professional, black-belt church rebuker uses this technique, it's usually so subtle and quick that you feel compelled to say a warm "thanks." Thanks for . . . well . . . ripping on me?

Some church rebukers specialize on certain topics. There was one guy at our church who people started calling "Calvin-nazi Ken." Somehow he turned every conversation into a confrontation against your beliefs on predestination. For those who know Reformation church history, John Calvin was notorious for his absurd rules, such as outlawing music, big hair, even the color red. Of course, Bob wasn't quite this bad. But he'd go so far as to stop you in the middle of your prayer, "Uh, Peter . . . that's not a

Some Christians have acquired the misguided notion that believers are called to confront the entire universe and do so in some freaky-weird ways.

correct prayer," as if John Calvin were looking down (or up) with frustrated disdain.

Just to mess with him, my friends started praying, "Lord, thank you for predestining me to believe prayer actually changes things." But really, it wasn't Bob's theology that bugged them. It was the fact that everyone knew he didn't seem to give a rip about anybody but himself. If someone's marriage was failing, his top priority would still be to convert them to all five points of Calvinism.

Don't misunderstand me; I do believe in healthy confrontation. And that's what we're going to talk about in this chapter. As the old saying goes, "People don't care how much we know until they know how much we care." In fact, according to Scripture, it's not truth that changes people, it's loving truth (1 Cor. 13:2).

Some Christians have acquired the misguided notion that believers are called to confront the entire universe and do so in some freaky-weird ways. And yes, if we love people, we will tell them that the stove is hot. However, a closer look at Scripture will reveal a more thoughtful approach to changing our world. But before we study it, allow me to share a concept with you called the checkbook theory.

HOW TO MAKE A LOVE SANDWICH

The checkbook theory has many names. In his best-selling book *The 7 Habits of Highly Effective People*, Stephen Covey called it an emotional bank account. Others call it a love sandwich, but that name creeps me out. Here's the gist: People are like checking accounts. You've got to make deposits before you can make withdrawals. If you write a check you cannot cash, it's called bouncing a check. (You see, young people, in the old days people actually got punished for spending money they didn't have. Sounds like a very scary world, doesn't it?) Banks would sometimes fine you fifty dollars for writing checks with insufficient funds. So, the analogy goes, if you confront someone (make a withdrawal) without first loving on them (making a deposit), you'll certainly make them mad (bounce a check). You should be able to do an amazingly intense confrontation without a person freaking out, provided that you've made an adequate amount of deposits of love. After all, these deposits reveal your love for them.

> *You should be able to do an amazingly intense confrontation without a person freaking out, provided that you've made an adequate amount of deposits of love.*

For example, we've all been confronted by people who didn't give a rip about us. And not surprisingly, we all responded in the same way, "Who are YOU to tell ME I shouldn't pee in a public shower?" or something similar. We all hate it when people share truths without first giving us empathy or showing us that they care. And why? We live in a culture where people share truths for selfish reasons all the time.

Honestly, we all operate with this conditional teachability as a matter of survival. Depending on the source, I've read that the average person experiences between six hundred and three thousand advertisements per day. Regardless of the *exact* number, we can all agree that a ton of ads bombard us each day. We live in a world where things are constantly being marketed to us: "You need this new car/wardrobe/electronic gadet/etc." "Your life will

> *We live in a world of endless truth claims. All throughout church history we see that even biblical truth has been constantly peddled for selfish gain.*

be better if you do a colon cleanse." We live in a world of endless truth claims. Throughout church history we see that even biblical truth has been constantly peddled for selfish gain. Our emotions protect us from such liars by conditioning our teachability. We all secretly ask, "Does this person really care about me? Will he inconveniently show me selfless love? Or is he just trying to take advantage of me, sucker me into a colon-cleanse?"

As a general rule, if you're ever scared to confront a certain person, ask yourself, "Have I made an adequate amount of deposits?" or "Have I shown them the type of love that they can understand?" If not, there's often a good reason why you're scared. You know you're about to bounce a check. Any idiot can share the truth, but earning the right to share truth is a totally different issue.

When applied to parenting, it can be profound. Your household can operate with an amazing number of high standards provided that your deposits of intelligible love exceed your demands. Thus, when kids rebel from their "Pharisee Parents," it's usually not a result of stringent boundary making. After all, I know many parents who are incredibly restrictive, yet their strong-willed kids never rebel for long. Rather, rebellion is usually the child's way of saying, "Your love isn't translating into my language; therefore, all I see is oppressiveness."

Throughout Scripture, we see God using the checkbook theory. Just think about the story of Zacchaeus (Luke 19), or the time Jesus ministered to the woman at the well (John 5). It was a massive gesture of kindness that He was even willing to talk to a woman like her in public. In fact, Jesus was so committed to making loving deposits that, despite the church rebukers of His day, He constantly risked His own reputation to hang out with tax collectors and sinners (Luke 5:27). "While we were still sinners, Christ died for us" (Rom. 5:8). "We love because he first

> *Your household can operate with an amazing number of high standards provided that your deposits of intelligible love exceed your demands.*

loved us" (1 John 4:19). "God's kindness leads [us] towards repentance" (Rom. 2:4).

It's also interesting to note that Jesus constantly healed people (demonstrating the mercy of heaven) while He preached truth. And when a person alters your life with such profound grace, you're likely to listen to him even if he has tough things to say to you. A person who makes adequate deposits never has to water down the truth. Jesus simply demonstrated the deposits of heaven, such as healing and deliverance, before He demanded submission.

But what about all the intense messages Jesus directed toward religious people? Did He use the checkbook theory then? I believe He did. When a religious person chronically forgets that they too are a sinner saved by grace, there's nothing left to do but judge (see Heb. 10:26). Of course, Jesus could do this because He was the perfect Son of God. However, if you and I start judging like this, we're likely to make a few mistakes. That's why James said, "There is only one Lawgiver and Judge" (James 4:12). After all, sinful human beings have a sketchy track record with this kind of stuff.

THE RISE OF THE ANGRY CHIPMUNKS

When our church started growing super fast, I had a pastor friend tell me, "Peter . . . you better get ready, because there are a lot of Christians who are going to judge your church just because its growing." In fact, he even said that Substance is going to become a swear word amidst struggling churches.

At first I thought, "No Way! I mean, why would that happen? Certainly, people are going to celebrate all of our crazy stories of transformation!" But my friend's advice was like a light switch. Within days, word started getting back to me about pastors who were saying the meanest things about our church and our motives. Many of the accusations didn't have any basis to them. Some of them were completely contradictory.

Someone called me anticharismatic. Then the very next week I was ironically called hypercharismatic. Based on the criticisms that kept coming back, I was a living paradox. You'd think I was a living theological contradiction. One person started a huge rumor that I was a "health and wealth" preacher because I said that "Jesus came that we might have life to the fullest," a direct quotation from John 10:10. We finally proved that rumor wrong when people started realizing that most of our executives had missing hubcaps on their rusted-out cars. Dealing with Christians like these is like being nibbled to death by a bunny rabbit.

One dude even told me, "You've got to be a compromised church if you feel the need to go with a weird name like Substance." He talked as though the Holy Spirit only falls on churches named after trees and rivers. Perhaps if we put all of these anointed names into one single moniker, we'd undergo unstoppable revival. "Welcome to Maple-Wood-Oak Creek-Birch-Elm-Fellowship River Church!" Boom! Instant revival!

However, the most irritating critique came from an article in a Christian newspaper. The headline read, "Substance: a church for itching ears." It was all about churches who compromise the gospel to reach people. Keep in mind, we're the church that did a four-part series on hell during Easter. So it's rather hard to make the argument that we water anything down. Of course, the article didn't address anything specific that we could respond to. Some of our friends, who apparently knew the author, told me that he wrote this even though he had never once visited our church or even listened to a single sermon.

Have you ever felt so demoralized that you just wanted to beat someone up in the name of Jesus? I always imagined in heaven that God would give me the opportunity to face my opponents in a pro-wrestling ring. Suddenly, I'm on a tag-team with GI Jesus. We march into the arena while the song "To hell with the Devil" pumps out of the speakers. Then, after Jesus pulls out a flawless gospel pile-driver on my opponent, I'd jump up onto the turn-buckle. And then I'd yank out my signature belt of truth, fold it, and give it a good snap to the chants of a roaring crowd, "Je-sus! Je-sus! Je-sus!"

As this whining fantasy continued, the Lord suddenly stole me from my victory slam to rebuke me, "Peter, do you really think you have it that hard?" I felt conviction all over instantly. I've done a large amount of work with pastors throughout the Middle East. The opposition they face makes mine look like an angry chipmunk. The Lord finally led me to read Luke 4 and 5, where Jesus went to minister in His hometown. Honestly, I've never seen church rebukers the same.

CALL OUT THE BEARS

If there was ever a group you'd hope would think the best about you, you'd expect it be your friends and family. Nothing better than a hometown crowd, right? But guess what the alleged God-seekers tried to do to Jesus? They tried to throw Him off a cliff! They attempted to murder Him in the name of defending God. (I bet they feel pretty stupid right now.)

Christ managed to escape, but this must have had a massive impact on Him. I don't know if you have ever survived an attempted murder. But I'd expect Him to be dealing with post-traumatic stress disorder. Jesus was God, but the human side of Him had to be grieving. Every one of His emotions were tested. I'm certain that this was one of those turning points. The people He grew up with tried to kill Him. If that had been me, it would have taken me decades to get over it.

Yet, immediately after this, Jesus went to Capernaum. He tried to get away to a solitary place to pray, which is exactly what I would do after people tried to kill me. And yet, these spiritual people were so invasive that they hunted Him down on His spiritual retreat and tried to lecture Him on His priorities.

Immediately after this, Jesus healed a paralytic, and some Pharisees started calling Him a blasphemer (Luke 5:21). Later, Jesus ministered to tax collectors (Luke 5:27); yet, along came the defenders of religious purity who started falsely calling Him a drunkard and a sinner. It almost seems like the gospel writer was trying to show that the perfect preacher on earth had constant criticism from people who saw themselves as defending authentic biblical faith.

As if Luke hadn't already made his point abundantly clear, Jesus started getting harassed by John the Baptist's disciples in the very next story. If there was ever a group you'd hope would leave you alone . . . if there was ever a group you'd think would assume the best . . . you'd hope it'd be your cousin's group—your cousin, of all people! But even they started nit-picking.

"Why aren't you fasting?" they asked. They wanted to know, "Why don't you seek God the way we think people should be seeking God?" Then, in the very next story, Jesus was ripped on for how He interpreted the Sabbath! The debates just never seemed to end. There had to have been a point where Jesus just wanted to freak out.

I'm certain Jesus thought about the passage in the Old Testament where the prophet Elisha was going up to Bethel (2 Kings 2). People started profaning God by mocking the prophet Elisha, saying, "Go on up, Baldy!" (And those of you who are going bald will appreciate this.) Elisha finally turned around and pronounced judgment on them. At his word, two bears suddenly came running out of the woods and mauled forty-two of them.[28]

So you can bet Jesus' disciples were like, "Jesus, there's got to be a team of bears nearby! Just do it." If God did this to protect Elisha, He'd certainly do it for Jesus. And guess what? Jesus knew this. That's why Jesus rebuked Peter when He was being betrayed, "Do you think I cannot call on my Father, and he will at once put at my disposal more than twelve legions[29] of angels?" (Matt. 26:53). Instead of calling out for angels and bears, Jesus even sought to reach His most ruthless persecutors, performing a miracle by healing a man's ear.

And there's a reason why Christ was so diligent in making deposits. As you'll see in the following story, this principle of the checkbook theory has a pretty profound effect on our ability to influence those around us.

TWO CONFRONTATIONS, TWO RESULTS

We once had a church rebuker who looked like Brutus from *Popeye the Sailorman*. She was the ultimate church rebuker, carrying the strength of ten men in the form of a She-man. An e-mail from her would cause the hairs on your neck to turn away in terror. You were almost guaranteed to get rebuked by her at some point. But what made her dangerous was the fact that so many people submitted to her dominion.

Along came an innocent young lady who had just started coming to our church. She was quite new in her faith. And she had a large amount of residue from her former way of life. We were patient with her. She had a flair for wearing a rather scant amount of clothing, yet we felt like God wanted to deal with one thing at a time. She had recently made some colossal lifestyle changes. Simply seeing her in church was already a miracle. We knew it was only a matter of time before God starting filing down her other rough spots.

But along came Brutus the confronter lady. Only a few Sundays after the girl started coming, she swooped down like a bird of prey. Brutus had never met the young lady before, but she didn't hesitate to lecture the girl over her inappropriate clothing. Within minutes, a few words turned into a shouting match. Not surprisingly, the young lady stopped coming.

Thankfully, my wife had built an amazing relationship with this young believer. The girl worked down at the local coffee shop. Soon all of her coworkers heard about the crazy lady at our church who belonged in the Taliban. Time and time again my wife was there for her, even financially. After things settled down, the girl eventually decided to come back to our church. However, this time, she stayed close to my wife, who promised to ward off the crazy lady.

Of course, that Sunday the young girl came dressed in an outfit that would have made Lady Gaga blush. We knew we needed to talk to her about it. We wondered, though, what she would do if we offended her? She blatantly disagreed with every argument that the church confronter lady gave, and the last thing we wanted to do was hurt her again. Yet she was attracting all of the wrong guys. We knew there was something deeper she was masking with her dress.

Finally, my wife just got blunt with her, "Honey, what in the world are you doing with your outfits? What kind of attention are you trying to get?" Stunned by my wife's tough love, the girl immediately started crying. After a powerful confession filled with childhood traumas and insecurities, she finally said to my wife, "Carolyn, I completely trust you. You're absolutely right. Would you help me change this?" You see, despite all of our fears, the girl responded to my wife's confrontation with total devotion.

What impacted me most about this easy confrontation was the contrast between my wife and the church-confronter lady. Both of them shared the exact same truth yet netted totally different results. What gives? Quite simply, it was the checkbook theory. My wife had made an amazing number of deposits. The confronter lady had made none. My wife earned the right to teach truth. The confronter lady tried to take a shortcut. God will, ultimately, hold her responsible for it.

Again, if the goal is simply to proclaim truth, then we're free to take all the shortcuts we want. But if the goal is to actually influence people with the truth, then we need to be aware of mankind's natural defense mechanisms.

LAZY LOVE

People always ask me why we have so many people converting to Christianity from crazy lifestyles. "How did you get so many ex-drug dealers into your church? . . . What kinds of messages do you preach that create this reaction?" Yet what people fail to understand is this: Christianity is not a message; it's a lifestyle. It's caught, not taught. It's the context of the message that matters. Yet diseased Christians are so idolatrously committed to their church-service formulas that they can't ever imagine an answer that isn't "preach more expository messages" or "do more prophetic altar ministry" (or whatever their narrow-minded key to revival is).

Truth was never meant to be delivered outside of the context of a loving community. By its very nature, it can only create rebellion

Christianity is not a message; it's a lifestyle. It's caught, not taught.

in the hearts of people who hear it. This is exactly what the apostle Paul was trying to say in Romans 7 and 8.

Paul teaches that although the Law (the truth) is holy, righteous, and good, it fails to transform people. It reveals our ugliness without the power or the hope of ever changing it. Only a relationship with the Law *and* the Spirit of life in Christ Jesus will set you free (Rom. 8:1–2). This relationship comes by fellowshiping with other people who live in Christ and, thus, are made one by His Holy Spirit.

Yet diseased Christians are so idolatrously committed to their church-service formulas that they can't ever imagine an answer that isn't "preach more expository messages" or "do more prophetic altar ministry" (or whatever their narrow-minded key to revival is).

As I mentioned in chapter three, one of the greatest statistical predictors of spiritual growth is how many intimate Christian friends you have at any given time.[30] It's not how many sermons you've heard or how many tears you've cried during worship. Those who study behavior modification clinically in the Christian context understand that your relational community affects your behavior far more than mere Bible knowledge or worship experiences.

Statistically, you can take two people, give them the same quantity of God's Word, and the one with the most Christian friends will be the one who's most likely to apply it. So the real question we need to ask ourselves is this, "Are we intimately connected with other people in the body of Christ?" If not, it doesn't matter how many sermons or worship experiences you ingest. You have very low odds of actually changing.

People who preach truth outside the context of loving community

People who preach truth outside the context of loving community are like child abusers who try shoving the steak of God's Word down a baby's throat.

are like child abusers who try shoving the steak of God's Word down a baby's throat. They produce death because they fail to comprehend how biblical repentance is created (Rom. 2:4). And adding insult to injury, they often self-righteously defend their authority to speak without making deposits.

> *Sadly, we will give an account for every needless spiritual death created by our haste-filled proclamations.*

Sadly, we will give an account for every needless spiritual death created by our haste-filled proclamations. And much of what we thought was persecution was really our own negligence.

But the good news is it doesn't have to be this way. Almost everyone in your city is teachable by someone. The question is: Are they teachable to you? Speaking truth is easy, but earning the right to speak truth is quite another.

You don't need to water down your gospel if you have enough deposits. Nor do you need to become one of those foolish Christians who parrot silly phrases like "the gospel is offensive," a statement that is often used as a cover-up for lazy love. Indeed, a relevant gospel isn't the subtraction of truth; rather, it's the addition of practical love.

We will sometimes spend countless hours depositing into a person's soul, and they will still reject us. The checkbook approach doesn't guarantee teachability where deception reigns. What it does guarantee is you will look like Christ. And frankly, isn't that the ultimate goal?

CHAPTER FOUR IN REVIEW

Key Ideas

1. Any long-term member of the body of Christ can get cynical about God's people.

2. According to Scripture, it's not truth that changes people but *loving truth*.

3. People are like checking accounts. You've got to make deposits before you make withdrawals.

4. Emotions protect us from liars by conditioning our teachability.

5. When a person alters your life with profound grace, you're likely to listen to him even if he has tough things to say to you.

6. The principle of the checkbook theory has a profound effect on our ability to influence those around us.

7. If our goal is to actually influence people with the truth, then we must be aware of mankind's natural defense mechanisms.

8. Christianity is not a message; it's a lifestyle.

9. Your relational community affects your behavior far more than mere Bible knowledge or worship experiences.

10. Speaking truth is easy; earning the right to speak truth is another thing.

Discussion Questions

1. Can you think of any past confrontations that went badly? How might the checkbook theory have affected these situations?

2. Authentic believers love the truth. If your love for the truth reveals the quality of your relationship with God, what is the quality of that relationship?

3. How does your relationship with God affect your teachability?

4. Who are you trying to influence? And what are some ways you could make deposits into their love bank?

5. Who are those people who have altered your lifestyle? How are you altering the lifestyles of others?

6. It has been said that some people give and receive love differently. In other words, some people falsely think they're making deposits while the recipient perceives love in a completely different way. How might this love-language problem impact the effectiveness of the checkbook theory?

7. Why is it easier for Christianity to be a message than it is for it to be a lifestyle?

8. How might a church practice the checkbook theory on a corporate level? Or if applied on a national level, how might this approach affect how Christians are perceived in politics?

9. After reading about Christ's opposition in Luke 4 and 5, what could we learn about leadership in the body of Christ?

10. How are you earning the right to speak the truth into the lives of others?

CHAPTER FIVE

Christians vs. Children of God

How are we supposed to love spooky, weird, or boring churches?

I LIVE ON A STREET WHERE people love to call the police for everything. If someone forgets to grab a bag of leaves from their front lawn, it suddenly becomes a public safety hazard. I like to think of myself as being a great neighbor. Yet, I've had my share of municipal violations—usually for cars parked on the street overnight or nonbiodegradable leaf bags. I'm still bitter that they shut down my backyard wood-chopping contest, and I'm surprised more of my neighbors didn't appreciate the Fourth of July when we played tag using bottle rockets and Roman candles. But, all in all, my neighbors are just looking out for me. Deep inside, there's a small part of me that feels loved, albeit a very small part.

I laugh when I read the police report in our local newspaper. It usually lists all of last month's crimes and complaints. One of them literally read as follows: "Complainant reported neighbor's dog was left outside for days at a time. Complainant was concerned for dog's well-being. Located dog in question and found it to be a statue."

A statue? I try to imagine how this neighbor felt upon realizing it was a statue. Perhaps this person thought, *You know, I always thought that dog was rather disciplined!* (In this neighbor's defense, the police could have arrested the statue owner for having poor taste.) Nevertheless, judging our neighbors can be tricky because we don't often see things correctly, do we?

Keep in mind: There's a difference between judging and discerning. When we judge, we often assume we know a person's motives. But only God can accurately judge hearts. That's probably why God's Word repeatedly tells us to leave judgment to Him.

"Do not judge, or you too will be judged. For in the same way you judge others, you will be judged" (Matt. 7:1–2). "There is only one Lawgiver and Judge, the one who is able to save and destroy. But you—who are you to judge your neighbor?" (James 4:12). "Speak and act as those who are going to be judged by the law that gives freedom, because judgment without mercy will be shown to anyone who has not been merciful. Mercy triumphs over judgment" (James 2:12–13).

The Bible also says that there is a time when judgment is necessary, such as predatory sin in the church (1 Cor. 5). If you struggle with alcohol, it's one thing. But if you take some youth-group kids out to get drunk, it's quite another issue. If Christians fail to take a stand in these circumstances, then God will actually hold us accountable for our inactivity.

Many Christians fail to realize that there is a clear pattern for biblical confrontation. For instance, if you have a problem with someone, healthy confrontation should always be done gently and with humility (Gal. 6:1–5). It must be done quickly so that it doesn't cause you to fester or spew on other people (Matt. 5:24; Heb.12:14–15). You need to go to the source of the problem first before you involve others (Matt. 18:15). So the time you confronted your spouse on *The Jerry Springer Show* probably wasn't the best idea. Even more, the Bible calls us to assume the best about others until proven guilty (1 Cor. 13:7). Only after these steps have been exhausted should a person involve others (Matt. 18:16) and then finally go public with their the grievance (v. 17). Even then, the audience shouldn't be a non-Christian audience (1 Cor. 6:1), which again probably means no to Jerry Springer. Besides, wisdom from heaven (as opposed to hell) is "peace-loving, considerate, submissive, full of mercy and good fruit, impartial and sincere" (James 3:17).

To be honest, a huge number of Christian blog posts, sermons, books, and Web sites wouldn't even pass the James 3:17 test. Much of what passes for accountability in the body of Christ is nothing more than demonic critique as we often take our confrontational approaches from the world rather than Scripture. Their actions reveal that their real master is the Accuser of others, a fancy name for the devil. As a result, churches are often sucked into gang warfare and doctrinal feuds that leave everyone feeling dirty.

Much of what passes for accountability in the body of Christ is nothing more than demonic critique as we often take our confrontational approaches from the world rather than Scripture.

Many of the people who destroy the body of Christ, ironically, do so under the pretense that they're protecting it. All of us participate in this seemingly spiritual process at some point or another. And part of this shocking revelation occurred to me when I stumbled upon a peculiar text in Genesis.

RE-EVALUATING THE GARDEN OF EDEN

Genesis 2:9 teaches us, "In the middle of the garden were the tree of life and the tree of the knowledge of good and evil." These two distinct trees existed at the center of this garden and are very important to this story. We are told that God gave Adam and Eve the ability to eat any fruit with one exception. They could not eat from the tree of the knowledge of good and evil.

As the story goes, a serpent offered Eve the chance to be like God if she were to eat fruit from this tree that God had explicitly said to steer clear of. She first resisted but later gave in to the serpent's logic that eating this fruit would not be a bad thing but would make her like God. Then Adam also ate the fruit, and both ushered sin into the world, which separated us from our Creator. This is what we mean when we talk about the fall of mankind. Everything has been going downhill for us ever since.

As a younger Christian, it was hard for me to rid my mind of the cartoonish image of Adam and Eve standing around with apples and fig leaves. So after reading this text as an adult, there were three things that struck me as profound:

1. This Wasn't a Normal Tree

Remember, this was a knowledge tree. And what are we ingesting when we eat from a knowledge tree? We ingest worldviews. We ingest ideologies and information. A knowledge tree is similar to a textbook, a library, or the Internet. Over the years, I've gotten so caught up in the Sunday school image of this as a literal fruit tree that I've missed a profound point. Seeking knowledge apart from God's presence and life results in death. Hold onto this concept as we explore two others.

2. The Temptation Appealed to Eve's Desire to Be Like God

We all want to be more like our heroes, don't we? Young people dress like their favorite rock stars. Little kids emulate every word of their parents (even words we hope they never hear). Likewise, I believe the devil saw this same positive desire in Adam and Eve. They wanted to be like their Heavenly Father. Yet the devil exploited this desire to a destructive end. It's similar to the crusades of the Middle Ages. Many Christians were lured into killing others under the pretense that it would make them more like Christ. The devil specializes in creating false paths to godliness. In fact, that's actually a good definition for religious sin, a plan to achieve godliness that goes beyond God's parameters.

3. It Wasn't Just Evil Knowledge That Led to Death

Rather, good knowledge also rests at the source of all sin: rape, genocide, torture, lying, gossip, and so on. I realize that it almost sounds like a paradox. How can good knowledge result in death?

One time I got into a spat with my wife. Anyone who's been married for any period of time will understand what I'm talking about. And in this particular argument, I was absolutely positive that I was right. I was determined to prove my *rightness* no matter what the cost.

I remember that final moment when I finished the perfect argument. I felt like Tom Cruise's character in *A Few Good Men*. As I started basking in my glory, she stormed off and didn't want to talk to me! What? Part of me expected her to stay . . . perhaps smile at my brilliance. I thought at least I'd get a "thank-you" for leading her back to the truth.

Over the years I've learned a profound marital lesson: You can win the battle yet still lose. The same is true with God. Rightness and godliness aren't always synonymous. You might be able to argue that you are *technically* right, but if you're not in sync with God, you're actually wrong.

THE FORNICATION FIGHTER

I remember a similar example from back when I was in college at the University of Minnesota. When the spring thaw came around, it wasn't uncommon to have tens of thousands of people walk through the open-air mall in between the imposing forum-like buildings.

One afternoon, I saw a crowd of students gathering around one angry man who was shouting at everyone. He was the only man wearing a suit and bow tie. And by the time I got close enough, I realized that he was pointing at people and calling them masturbators.

Now, I've yelled at people before—like when an official makes a terrible call at a sports game—but I never remember shouting "masturbator." Maybe I need to be more creative in my name-calling, but something told me this wasn't a good situation.

With a rather dramatic flair, the man pointed at various people around him and screeched, "You prostitutes, drunkards, and homosexuals! None of you will inherit the kingdom!" His young son stood nearby wearing a sandwich board depicting a person burning in hell. People were walking away dejected saying, "Why are Christians so mean?" I had been sharing Christ with numerous people in my dormitory, and it broke my heart to see many of them nearby with disillusioned looks on their faces.

So allow me to ask you an obvious question: Do you think this man brought anyone closer to God? No. Because he was blatantly ignoring Paul's advice in 2 Corinthians 3:6 that God has "made us competent as ministers of a new covenant—not of the letter but of the Spirit; for the letter kills, but the Spirit gives life."

As I mentioned before, the devil can hijack truth when it's delivered from an unloving heart or out of self-righteousness. Again, "wisdom from heaven" (as opposed to hell) is "peace-loving, considerate, submissive, full of mercy and good fruit, impartial and sincere" (James 3:17). This means that, if we share truth in a way that is void of these characteristics, we might be technically right but still not be life-giving.

That's why when my wife saw what was happening with this crazy mall preacher, she literally threw down her books and went right out to the man and confronted him. A few people even cheered as she did it. I'm certain that this is how the people of Jesus' day felt when someone had the guts to take on the religious establishment.

Whether you think she did the right thing or not, I don't want you to miss my greater point: You can have correct theology and not be in step with God (Matt. 23:3). That was one of the major lessons of the Fall (Gen. 3). It's okay to want to be like God, but there is a right and wrong way to be like Him. Good knowledge (aka correct theology), such as the knowledge found in the forbidden tree, doesn't necessarily lead us to life. And in the New Testament, we see this contrast when Jesus asks us to become like "little children."

For example, in Matthew 19:13–14, we see all sorts of little kids running to Jesus, hoping that He'd place His hands on them and pray for them. "But," Matthew records, "the disciples rebuked those who brought them. Jesus said, 'Let the

> *You can have correct theology and not be in step with God.*

little children come to me, and do not hinder them, for the kingdom of heaven belongs to such as these.' When he had placed his hands on them, he went on from there."

Jesus seems to be saying that the realities of heaven belong to those who run to God like these kids. Even more, these kids were hoping that Jesus would bless them—a childish, perhaps even self-centered, act to a religious person. Yet, Jesus completely disagreed. He essentially countered that God loves it when we seek His blessings.

God doesn't want us to become a bunch of self-centered consumers who treat Him like a cosmic Santa Claus. Too many Christians have been suckered into "prosperity gospels" or the American dream rather than God's dream. But, at the same time, God also doesn't want us to become cynical, lemon-faced adults who are upset at other Christians because they won't wear our favorite crown of thorns. In fact, God gets irritated when we stop seeing Him as the one who "rewards those who earnestly seek him" (Heb. 11:6).

One of my favorite things to do is worship with little kids. They don't seem to complicate worship as many adults do. My three kids constantly want me to crank up the stereo and dance with them. When they were little, no matter what song I'd put on, they'd lift up their hands and yell, "I love you, God!" (which got a bit strange when "Ladies Night" started playing—but they didn't care). No matter how depressed I was feeling, my burdens seemed to be lifted as I jumped around with them. Suddenly, God was my Father again (Matt. 6:8). He was my protector (Ps. 91). I didn't have to take care of my needs because my Daddy would be there to help.

You can understand why Jesus was irritated with His disciples in Matthew 19, especially when a chapter earlier Jesus had already taught them: "Unless you change and become like little children, you will never enter the kingdom of heaven" (Matt. 18:3). Jesus wasn't threatening them. It was simply a statement of fact. Grace cannot invade a self-sufficient heart. God cannot be our Father if we refuse to be His kids. Too often we choose to

Cynicism is a sure sign that someone has robbed you of your innocence.

be Christians rather than children of God. Cynicism is a sure sign that someone has robbed you of your innocence.

That's why, in the New Testament, there are two different ways to be like God. The first and healthiest approach is that we simply surrender to the kingdom of heaven. We acknowledge that we offer nothing of value. Once heaven invades our childlike worship, we are filled with the fruit of the Holy Spirit (Gal. 5:22–23). We didn't earn it through adultish acts of religion. We simply ingested Christ, the bread of life (John 6:35). And suddenly, Christ came to live in us (Col. 1:27)!

In direct contrast, we see the Adam-and-Eve approach to being like God. We study the knowledge of good and evil. We study right and wrong theology, right and wrong moral behavior. And through this knowledge we talk the talk, yet there's a blaming spirit that accompanies it (Gen.3:12). We take on the appearance of godliness, yet it rarely reflects the fruit of the Holy Spirit. We share truth, but it's devoid of the "peace-loving, considerate, submissive" wisdom of heaven (James 3:17).

We've all met Christians who can spew theology, yet cynicism runs rampant below the surface. We've all heard sermons that oppressed us instead of uplifted us. Quite often it's because we're still trying to achieve spirituality through the same tree that messed us up in the first place.

And it's not like God didn't want us to learn about good and evil. Rather, He wanted us to discern these things without the caustic instinct to be the judge of creation, a role that was exclusively reserved for Him (James 4:12).

This faulty approach to godliness is what Jesus accused the Pharisees of doing when He said, "You diligently study the Scriptures because you think that by them you possess eternal life. These are the Scriptures that testify about me, yet you refuse to come to me to have life" (John 5:39–40). Jesus seems to be saying (according to the Peter Haas Translation), "You still seek knowledge of good and evil, as if somehow you'll reach God. But what you need is me! *I* am the bread of life, the tree of life, and the living water! Ingest me!"

So was Jesus saying that Bible reading can lead us astray? Yes, if it's divorced from Him and the Spirit of life that illuminates it. It is possible to seek God and use Scripture for all the wrong reasons.

> *It is possible to seek God and use Scripture for all the wrong reasons.*

One time, after I shared a devotional with a small group of people, my friend came up to me and said, "Uhh, Peter, there's no way that your idea came from the Bible!" I immediately got defensive. I suddenly felt like a grizzly bear getting kicked out of hibernation. I got all riled up. After all, I knew I was right. (And if you haven't noticed, I'm right a lot.) So I immediately began searching Scripture so I could say, "Oh yeah? Check this out, you dork! Apparently, *you* are the one who doesn't know the Bible!"

So let me ask you another obvious question: Was I reading my Bible so that I could uplift my brother? Not at all. I just wanted to show him that he's an idiot who's making my life harder. Likewise, I'm not always convinced that we're reading and preaching Scripture in order to love and uplift people more.

Much like the Pharisees, many Christians study the Bible with ill motives. For some, it's that they serve an idol called "perfect theology." It comforts them to feel like they have everything figured out. After all, if they can squeeze God into their systematic theology, they no longer have to fear Him. He's tame and predictable. They can relax because the lion is finally put in a cage, which is why they're so threatened by anyone who wrestles with their assumptions. Others use the Bible to control others or to feel special. Still others preach because they feel victimized by other people's sin. Thus preaching becomes one of the few ways they feel they can strike back.

> *After all, if they can squeeze God into their systematic theology, they no longer have to fear Him.*

Just because Scripture may come from our mouths, it doesn't mean we're giving life to others.

And if we want to remain healthy followers of Christ, we've got to keep a few important things in mind:

CAUTION #1: IF YOU JUDGE BASED ON FORMAT OR STYLE INSTEAD OF FRUITFULNESS, YOU'LL MISS GOD

At my local Christian bookstore, there are a dizzying array of books ranting about the ideal church. They propose unsubstantiated conclusions like: Megachurches are all compromised; Home churches are God's favorite; God only moves in churches with free-flowing altar ministry; If it's not ultrarelevant, then it's not God; and so on. Almost all of these arguments tend to center around a formatting issue related to church sizes or church services. Certainly, a healthy debate is always beneficial, provided it's clothed in both research and humility. But even healthy debates can be a ridiculous exercise that misses a greater point. Let me show you one such example.

One of the great debates among leaders relates to church size. This discussion has been a longtime obsession of mine. I've spent a good amount of time wondering about the perfect church size.

In favor of small churches, there are a number of studies that show intimate community is the leading statistical predictor of spiritual transformation.[31] Church small groups are a virtual necessity for statistical health.[32] That's why our church constantly advocates small groups. It's not uncommon for Substance to have more people in small groups than those attending our services. Thus, one could easily conclude that smaller is better.

In direct contradiction to the smaller-is-better claim, though, are many studies showing that bigger is better. One study, ironically, found that you're more likely to have meaningful relationships that extend outside of church services in churches "over 1,000 members than those with less than this."[33] Even more, the most reliable studies show that the majority of church growth in the U.S. in the last twenty years occurred in churches with over 1,000 members. American churches between one hundred and one thousand members are having incredibly bad luck trying to grow.[34] Hence, one could easily assume that large churches are intrinsically better at evangelism.

But here's where both sides of this argument become silly. No one in their right mind would ever claim that a 1,900-square-foot, 3-bedroom, brick house produces healthier children. Why not? It's because bricks and mortar (i.e., the format of the house) ultimately have nothing to do with parenting. Rather, it's the *values* of the house that matter. Do mom and dad spend time with their kids? Do they demonstrate a healthy marriage with healthy communication? In other words, healthy family values transcend such superficial things as home size and building materials.

In the same way, no one would ever claim medium-sized churches have more faith than others, because we all know that faith, discipleship, and fellowship are values that operate independently of format. Church leaders either effectively provoke these values—regardless of church size or worship format—or they don't.

That's why Jesus steered believers away from judging a prophet (or church leader) based on format versus fruit (Matt. 7:18). Jesus got pretty upset when His disciples stopped another group from doing ministry because they didn't meet their expectations, a fancy way of saying they did things differently (Mark 9:38–41).

And we can understand Christ's irritation when this is the same reason why the Pharisees wouldn't accept Him as the Messiah. Jesus simply didn't fit the narrow-minded format that people were trained to see as healthy. So, naturally, He got a bit passionate when His own followers started doing the same thing.

We need to celebrate a diversity of church formats. Church formats are often an extension of a leader's gift mix and resources, not a divine cookie cutter by which all churches must be measured. Not all formats

> *Jesus got pretty upset when His disciples stopped another group from doing ministry because they didn't meet their expectations, a fancy way of saying they did things differently.*

of church are equally bearing fruit in the United States, or wherever you live. But let's not turn our opinions into the only way to be a real Christian.

> *Let's not turn our opinions into the only way to be a real Christian.*

Conviction in Strange Places

A while back, I was flipping through the channels and stumbled upon this one southern televangelist. Everything about him was rather irritating. His preaching style was filled with Christian buzzwords. His outfit looked as if he had just raided a 1980s suit factory. Even his voice made me want to start ripping on him. I sat there with pure cynicism flowing out of my heart.

And suddenly I sensed the voice of the Holy Spirit impressing on my heart, "Peter, shut up and listen! Because I've got something to say to you through this person!" It wasn't an audible voice. But it was the exact opposite of what I was thinking.

Immediately, I felt this holy fear of the Lord. Conviction was all over me. I instantly realized that I was lacking the fruit of the Holy Spirit (specifically kindness). So, right there on my couch, I repented and started listening to this preacher with a totally different attitude. Before long, the preacher shared a Scripture verse that jolted me! It was so powerful I started weeping.

I immediately became aware that my wife might walk around the corner at any given moment. I furiously started trying to wipe away the snot. But my hands were like a windshield wiper in a tidal wave. I wasn't going to be able to hide this one. Even though my wife knows that I regularly cry when I watch NFL films, having a similar experience watching this TV preacher would be weird. I knew she wouldn't understand.

It touched me so much because, for the previous month, I had been praying for a breakthrough in a specific area. And this was the exact word I needed to hear. In fact, over the years, many of my most profound God encounters have come from some pretty bizarre places.

CAUTION #2: WHEN YOU JUDGE, YOU BECOME ISOLATED FROM THE GRACE OF GOD IN OTHER PEOPLE

The apostle Peter begged us to love each other because our attitude toward one another makes up for many of our faults and mistakes. He knew that cynicism and critique can rip apart just about any congregation if we let it. No matter how great of a church you attend, you can bet that the devil is actively working to seed cynicism and critique.

Peter writes in his first epistle, "Each one should use whatever gift he has received to serve others, faithfully administering God's grace in its various forms" (1 Pet. 4:10). When Christians are not united, we are actually lacking the whole measure of God's grace in our lives.

Besides, most of the things that Christians divide over are actually kind of silly. That's why Jesus had to come in the first place. All of our feeble attempts to worship God are a bit ridiculous. Yet He still takes pleasure when we approach Him with childlike hearts.

So whenever I come upon forms of Christianity I disagree with, or churches that have worship that's weird to me, this is what I do: Rather than critiquing and nitpicking, I give them the benefit of the doubt. I say, "Father, what grace have you placed inside of them? Lord, how can I enjoy you through this person? They might wear way too much makeup or emphasize secondary doctrine way more than is healthy. Their worship may be mega-boring, mega-spooky, or mega-long, but that doesn't mean you can't still use them to accomplish your will."

Almost every time I pray this, something wild happens to me. Suddenly, I start to see them as God sees them. I can feel the grace of heaven. And then something powerful happens: When I look into their eyes, no matter how strange they appear to

When Christians are not united, we are actually lacking the whole measure of God's grace in our lives.

me, I'm truly able to say, "I love you!" And when I say it, they actually believe it because they feel God's love coming straight through me.

And once you have that kind of spiritual rapport, you can have amazing discussions that are free from arrogance or fear. You can communicate without anyone feeling defensive. The flow of conversation can go back and forth without all the emotions that often cloud the truth.

CAUTION #3: YOU CAN'T ANTAGONIZE AND INFLUENCE AT THE SAME TIME

I'm razzing a good number of approaches to Christianity in this book, but those who really know me will find that I'm actually quite warmhearted to Christians of all kinds. In fact, the approaches to Christianity that are strangest to us are often the ones that have the most to speak to us.

I'm not suggesting that we open up our hearts to anyone or anything that claims to be Christian. (No snake handling. Seriously, people!) But I believe that God can speak to us in all sorts of ways, we can stay free in the innocence of Christ and, lastly, God can use us to reach all sorts of people. I'm convinced that if we can keep all three of these attributes flowing in our lives, our churches will finally be prepared to see an unstoppable revival in our generation.

CHAPTER FIVE IN REVIEW

Key Ideas

1. There's a difference between judging and discerning.
2. Many people who destroy the body of Christ do so under the pretense that they're protecting it.
3. When we eat from a knowledge tree, we ingest worldviews, ideologies, and information.
4. Religious sin is a desire for godliness that goes beyond God's plan.

5. Truth can be used for demonic purposes when it's delivered outside of God's timing and void of love.

6. You can have correct theology but not be in step with God.

7. Grace cannot invade a self-sufficient heart.

8. There's a healthy and unhealthy way to become more like God—simply surrender to the kingdom of heaven or study right and wrong theology and moral behavior.

9. If you judge others, you become isolated from the grace of God in other people.

10. You can't antagonize and influence at the same time.

Discussion Questions

1. Have you ever had someone complain about you to someone else without coming to you first? How did it make you feel? According to Matthew 18:15, are there any circumstances where you should go to someone else other than the person you have a problem with?

2. Describe a time when you committed religious sin. At what point did you detour from God's plan?

3. According to James 3:17, how should we deal with books, blogs, pastors, or Web sites that defame specific Christians?

4. How would God prefer you share truth with another believer?

5. Self-sufficiency blocks grace in the life of a believer. Are you suffering from self-sufficiency or living in grace? How do you know?

6. Looking back over the last decade of your life, have you ever held a strong opinion about church methods that you changed your opinion on? If so, what was it? And how have you changed?

7. If you were to rate your cynicism about church on a scale of one to ten (with ten being extremely cynical), where would you be? And why?

8. Why do you think people get so locked into one church model as the correct model? How do you think your season of life

influences the model of church you prefer? (For example, how might being single, having kids, or becoming a senior citizen affect your criteria?)

9. The media often reports on the public protests of people who claim to be believers but espouse hate on others. What does this radical demonstration of hatred do to people who are pursuing God for the first time?

10. Why is it so hard for God's love to penetrate the hearts of people who have been the object of Christian hatred?

CHAPTER SIX

The Art of
Hedge Making

*What are the classic behaviors of a
well-meaning legalist?*

Hᴀᴠᴇ ʏᴏᴜ ᴇᴠᴇʀ ꜱᴇᴇɴ ᴀɴ ᴜɴᴅᴇɴɪᴀʙʟᴇ miracle? I'm talking
about the kind that gives you goose bumps and makes you giddy like
a kid at a magic show. I've seen some pretty crazy stuff over the years.

Scripture seems to show that God has a dramatic bias toward
believers who live in unity with other believers. For example, the
Psalmist wrote, "When God's people live together in unity . . . there
the Lᴏʀᴅ bestows his blessing" (Ps. 133:1, 3). We learn from James
5:16 that healing is preceded by authentic agreement with other righteous believers. Or as a more popular example of this divine bias,
Jesus talks about a unique blessing, a power that God especially re-
serves for unity.

Jesus said, "Truly I tell you, whatever you bind on earth will
be bound in heaven . . . if two of you on earth agree about anything they ask for, it will be done for them by my Father in heaven"
(Matt. 18:18–19). Jesus was essentially saying that God gives special
privileges to Christians who live in prayerful agreement and unity.
We simply have more power together than when we seek God alone.
Perhaps this is why Christ was so disturbed that His closest friends
couldn't stay awake with Him to pray in the Garden of Gethsemane.

We read about the Tower of Babel in Genesis 11. God's people were rebelling against Him. They were trying to glorify themselves by building a great tower. Yet, despite their defiance, God paid them a pretty huge compliment, "If as one people speaking the same language they have begun to do this, then nothing they plan to do will be impossible for them" (v. 6). This seems to be the Old Testament version of Matthew 18:19. And if this is mankind's potential when defying God, can you imagine our potential with God on our side?

I had been discussing these texts with my leaders one night when many of them started lamenting the fact that they hadn't seen many undeniable miracles lately. One leader even confessed, "I don't know if I've ever seen a miracle like the kind of power mentioned in Matthew 18 that forces me to say: God is here."

And almost on cue, my cell phone interrupted our meeting. It was a young lady from our church. She was literally weeping on the phone. It turned out that she had just returned from the doctor, who had diagnosed her with a huge tumor. It had doubled in size since the previous week. She had a strong family history of cancer. So, quite naturally, she was freaking out.

The moment I got off the phone, my leadership team all stared at me with wide-eyed concern. "What happened?" one of my leaders inquired. I felt overwhelmed with the sense that God had a divine lesson for all of us. So I blurted, with inspirational boldness, "Well guys, today is your day to see a miracle! Team, we're going to fast all week for this girl! And as surely as I know the Lord, He's going to heal her."

Have you ever made a rash vow? Have you ever made a bold declaration that you had no ability to back up? After the meeting ended that evening, my faith suddenly sprung a leak. And by the next morning, my war cry turned into a miserable yelp. I started asking myself, "Did I get a bit presumptive in front of my team? I mean, God's Word constantly refers to Him as a healer, right?" But waiting on any answer to prayer can create a mental minefield of sorts. Even still, my team fasted with me. We were hungry to see God move.

The young lady went in for surgery at the end of the week. She, too, was filled with supernatural expectation. And whether God healed her or simply guided the surgeon's hands, it didn't matter to her. She simply knew that God was going to show up in response to our agreement.

Immediately before the surgery, the second set of X-rays revealed something dreadfully wrong. The nurses kept whispering to one another. The doctor looked concerned. Our young friend began wondering, "Is it worse than I thought?"

The doctor finally explained, "I'm sorry if I look mystified. But it's just that I'm comparing your new x-rays to those we took a few days ago and . . . although this is medically impossible, that huge tumor has completely disappeared." She was miraculously healed. And she had the undeniable X-rays to prove it.

The news spread quickly throughout our leadership team. The moment I heard this report, I did an end-zone dance and strutted like my faith never wavered. But deep inside I felt the Holy Spirit quipping at me, "Oh, you of leaky faith."

I'm not saying that if you live in the power of agreement that God will always do whatever we want in the timeline that we want it done. After all, God is God. He answers our prayers and deepest yearnings in diverse ways. And the Bible gives many reasons why we don't always get what we want.

Frankly, there are a lot of prayers that I'm actually glad He didn't answer—like the time I prayed that my mom would let me get a rattail at my next hair cut; or the time I asked God to help me afford a WWJD tattoo that I never got. Part of me wonders if heaven has a YouTube site showcasing all of the silly prayers we pray. Despite the fact that God doesn't always do what we want, we'd also be foolish if we denied the fact that God often shows up when we live in agreement and unity.

I recently read about a powerful citywide prayer meeting in Brazil. Due to a few powerful business owners, the meetings were forced to stop. Immediately after the meetings shut down, the city crime rates surprisingly jumped by over 50 percent. Indeed, the crime rates increased so dramatically within ninety days that both the mayor and chief of police begged for the prayer meetings to start again. And sure enough, the moment the meetings resumed, the crime rate suddenly dropped again. Even the secular newspaper credited prayer as the unmistakable difference maker. Since that time, church growth in that region has jumped by an unprecedented 37 percent (over a half million people started attending church again).[35]

So here is the million-dollar question: If God offers us so many miraculous incentives for living in unity, why don't we strive for it more? And why are so many churches and organizations bickering and splitting over the silliest stuff? We all get our priorities mixed up from time to time. So allow me to show you a few reasons why this happens.

THE BELIEF CONTINUUM

We all know that *not all beliefs are equally important*, right? For example, your opinion on "Coke vs. Pepsi" isn't as important as proclaiming, "Jesus is the Son of God!" Neither does your opinion on Bible translations compare to your opinion on the existence of heaven and hell. But if we fail to stratify them, we may end up starting wars over some pretty silly priorities.

After the Reformation hit Europe, it was a very easy time to lose your life for believing certain things from the Bible. In times of uncertainty, many people want to take gray areas of Scripture and make them black and white. This practice was the spark that caused thousands to become burned at the stake during the reformation. Thus, around 1627, a rather unknown author penned the famous expression, "Unity in what is essential. Liberty in non-essentials. And in all things, freedom."[36] His goal was to keep people from losing their heads (literally and figuratively). So allow me to introduce a quick diagram that illustrates this.[37]

The Belief Continuum

Theological or Moral...
Fundamentals . . . . Inferences . . . . Speculations . . . . . . Opinions

Essentials   **Non-Essentials**

On the far left side, we see the word *Fundamentals.* These are doctrines that most scholars throughout history have considered essential to biblical Christianity. For example, the divinity of Christ, the Resurrection, the existence of heaven and hell, the reliability of Scripture, and salvation through Christ alone are a few of the doctrines that, if altered, would fundamentally change the biblical and historical foundations of Christianity.

Fundamentals are usually based upon multiple proof texts. They are generally too black and white to make gray. Thus, anyone wanting to dismantle these doctrines has his work cut out for him.

Moving to the right, we find *Inferences.* The reason I use this word is because these types of doctrines can get a bit more hazy. They require us to infer things that go beyond the text in order to make sense of them. Inferences aren't supported by the same number of proof texts and traditions as fundamentals.

For example, many people debate the question: Does the Bible say that women can be in ministry? There are only a couple of texts that deal with this issue, most of which raise fascinating yet complicated questions about local context and interpretation.[38]

Personally, the debate is rather strange when almost 70 percent of the body of Christ is women. Thus, to bench such a significant group from preaching has the practical effect of grinding the entire Great Commission to a screeching halt. But despite my support of women preachers, at the very least, I can intellectually comprehend how certain groups could interpret these passages differently. In the end, inferences simply aren't as black and white when compared to many fundamentals.

Moving even further to the right are *Speculations.* These are doctrines based on numerous inferences from numerous parts of Scripture. For example, end-times doctrines (eschatology) or sovereignty doctrines (like predestination or free will) are classic examples of speculation. They generally require us to stack numerous biblical assumptions together, including many ideas and assumptions that go well beyond Scripture.[39]

Last, we find *Opinions* on the far right. People will eternally debate worship styles, what kinds of instruments should be played, how many songs, what types of songs, how much altar ministry, modesty issues, etc.

As we found out in chapter one, some people dislike long hair on men. Some Christians feel tattoos are evil (which is perhaps why God didn't answer my prayer the way I wanted Him to). For a season, I per-

> *Every human being has the sinful tendency to take their opinions, inferences, and speculations and pass them off as fundamentals.*

sonally believed that mullets grieved the Holy Spirit. And I'm still not convinced that the world needs Christian fortune cookies.

But, in light of these varying levels of belief, it's important to understand: Every human being has the sinful tendency to take their opinions, inferences, and speculations and pass them off as fundamentals. In some ways, there's an insecurity inside all of us that hates to have any beliefs that are less than certain. Indeed, the word *fundamentalism* is a term used to describe people who desire to make all of their speculations and opinions fundamental. And, as we'll soon learn, there are many reasons why people strive for this world of black and white.

AN ARGUMENT FOR HUMILITY

One time I was talking with a Christian who thought he knew everything about predestination. He kept making cocky statements as if it were so simple. And you've got to understand, this topic was a ten-year obsession for me. After reading an endless amount of scholarly literature on the topic, I devoted myself to memorizing over a hundred Bible passages related to the subject. My hope was that truth would curl up and die at my feet. In the end, the only discovery I made was that the entire issue comes down to a half dozen unknowable issues that go well beyond Scripture.

I still don't claim to understand the beginning of it, but I knew enough to know that this guy was totally full of himself. And his overconfidence was downright irritating. While resisting the urge to give him an intellectual spanking, my gentler side opted to take a different strategy, asking him, "Of all the knowledge that's available in the universe, how much do you think mankind even knows?" I then started explaining to him that our own small galaxy would take millions of years to cross at light speed. Yet astronomers have found clusters of galaxies numbering into the thousands, and human beings have yet to reach Mars. He started getting suspicious about my random rant. I finally asked him to quantify mankind's knowledge with a percentage. He admitted, "Well . . . If I exaggerate a bit, mankind probably doesn't even know one-billionth of a percent of what's out there."

Then I asked him, "And of all the knowledge that mankind knows, how much of that do you personally know? Think about all of the libraries on planet earth, then think about how much of those libraries that you know." He stood back and said, "Probably less than .000000001 percent of that."

"So, to summarize," I told him, "you and I are pretty much total and complete idiots—is that right?" He got my point. Much of our discussion was about things that went way beyond our ability to speak with confidence. My friend finally admitted that much of his overconfidence was merely emulating other overconfident preachers he was listening to.

Keep in mind, it's fine to be passionate about our Bible speculations—provided we have enough humility to publically admit where the issues get gray. As we grow more comfortable with our assumptions, we get increasingly intolerant of people who need to wrestle with them. Our motives behind making things black and white are usually good—we want to protect people. We want to undercut potentially hurtful debates in our church. Yet, as we'll see below, these good intensions can lead to some pretty devastating religious diseases if not kept in check.

> *As we grow more comfortable with our assumptions, we get increasingly intolerant of people who need to wrestle with them.*

OUR OBSESSION WITH SAFETY

Remember when playgrounds used to be dangerous? Way before woodchips and rubber mulch, we had a soft layer of concrete to buffer our falls. Playgrounds were the battlefield through which childhood warriors were made—where truth-or-dare led to bloody chins and broken hearts.

I have to laugh when I think about the person who created some of our favorite playground toys. Theoretically, teeter-totters are intended to create a leisurely up and down sensation, perhaps tricking children into a powerful lesson on teamwork. But I can't remember a single time when the true goal wasn't to see how high I could violently buck my opponent into the air. And the merry-go-round was a spinning torture device at the hands of older kids. Its entertainment factor consisted of flinging your dizzy siblings through the air. If successful, someone's little sister would hilariously vomit on the way back home.

Safety was a low priority in those days because playgrounds were a form of natural selection. Slides were built twelve feet high and had no side rails. Playgrounds served as a way of thinning out the herd.

When families were larger, we needed a way to get more attention from our parents; thus, if little sister didn't come home, we'd have less competition for the singular television set. Parents knew this and secretly wanted less competition as well; hence, they trusted us to go to the local playground alone. It was a temporary *Lord of the Flies* situation. Parents knew, however, we could always come home if a retreat was absolutely necessary.

One of my favorite games as a fifth grader was called ghost riding. We'd ride our dirt bikes up to the parallel bars; and, upon reaching the neck-high bar, we'd launch our bikes as hard as we could while jumping off of them. The goal was to see who could get their bike to roll as far as possible without anyone riding it. A talented ghost rider could sometimes achieve over seventy feet of rider-less pleasure.

It would inevitably end badly. Only on rare occasions would parents stop us. Either someone would clothesline themselves, surviving virtual decapitation; or, the bike itself would become a dangerous projectile to some unsuspecting four-year-old. It was quite dramatic because you could often see the impending collisions coming approximately ten seconds out.

Today's playgrounds are completely different. They are squishy, forgiving bubbles where parents make their kids slurp on sanitizing lotion. The world is a better place now that we aren't losing kids to rider-less bikes. But I think we're also becoming aware that overprotecting can also have its liabilities. There's a stunning amount of new research showing that overprotective parents produce less healthy kids.[40] There has to be a balance, and this idea of balance is something the Pharisees of Jesus' day got embarrassingly wrong.

HEDGES AROUND THE LAW

Pharisees were obsessed with hedges of protection—protective rules that buffered people from the mere possibility of sin. The Bible says, "Remember the Sabbath day by keeping it holy" (Ex. 20:8). Various groups created endless hedges or specific laws that doubly protected people from violating this law.

One modern day example might be to declare all movies are bad so that we ensure our children don't see movies with messages we don't agree with. One of my friends humorously recalls that his former church forbade premarital sex because it might lead to dancing. You get the idea. Hedges are intended to be a protective buffer. Too often, these hedges can be used to oppress people.

In Jesus' day, many teachers of the Law actually added over one hundred additional hedges to the Sabbath. So when we see Jesus and His disciples being accused of disobeying the Sabbath, Jesus obviously wasn't disobeying Scripture; rather, He was simply disobeying hedges (i.e., opinions that had been turned into fundamentals).

Hedges are intended to be a protective buffer. Too often, these hedges can be used to oppress people.

Even today, massive numbers of Israeli citizens forbid flipping light switches on the Sabbath or even touching elevator buttons as a hedge to prevent people from breaking the Sabbath. And I'm not implying anyone is currently forced to do it. For many of them, it's a joyful way to serve their God. But, in Jesus' day there would often be violent ramifications for simply disagreeing with a well-known teacher's interpretation.

However, Jesus never objected to taking radical measures to achieve purity. He, too, advocated, "If your eye causes you to sin, gouge it out" (Mark 9:47, NLT). That is to say, if you have to take radical steps to honor God, do it. And in a hedge-less culture like ours, we could probably stand to learn a bit more about this. Once you get to know me, I have many personal hedges that might seem a bit extreme to some. Having boundaries isn't the problem. It's when we force all of our personal convictions onto other people that things can get pretty weird.

Notice that Jesus didn't say, "If someone's eye causes them to sin, gouge it out *for them*." Again, it's important to remember that, on a communal level, Jesus advocated a minimal number of hedges (Matt. 11:30). And here are a few suggestions as to why He did this.

1. Hedge making often becomes a substitute for listening to the Holy Spirit or discerning God's will. It's way easier to tell teenagers all secular music is bad than to teach them spiritual discernment. Teaching people discernment requires far more work and much more risk. People also seem to lose their vigilance when an authority is willing to predigest it for them. And that leads to our second problem.

2. Hedge making causes people to seek God's Word less. Many pastors think I'm strange for saying this, but I actually enjoy a certain amount of theological tension in my church. There's nothing that drives people to Scripture more than theological tension. Most of us didn't give a rip about certain doctrines or theological issues until we, or someone we loved, started struggling with it.

That's why the best disciple makers are tension makers more than teachers. I regularly share my speculations and inferences; when I do, I make sure to add enough humility and soul tension so that

> *That's why the best disciple makers are tension makers more than teachers.*

it actually results in people seeking God more than old-fashioned indoctrination.

For example, I recently did a teaching series on the end-times doctrines. But rather than giving everyone a predigested opinion, I decided to share a detailed argument for all three major schools of thought, and then allow the people to decide for themselves. Don't get me wrong. I definitely had an opinion. At times, it was incredibly difficult for me to stay objective. Yet, I refused to rob people of their soul tension. The net result was an unprecedented number of people scouring their Bibles on a new level.

That's why I strategically keep our church's statement of faith exclusively limited to fundamentals while mixing in permissive statements on inferences and speculations. If our membership requirements screen out everyone who doesn't think like us, not only will we fail to influence outsiders but we'll inadvertently remove the very spark that drives us to explore God's Word. To put it plainly, homogenous groups of Christians seek indoctrination more than Scripture. So then, why do so many people seek it?

Theological tension can be very agitating, especially if those debating things are either arrogant or polarizing. To counteract this, insecure churches unfortunately respond by stamping out a counterfeit type of unity—a unity through uniformity of thought rather than unity through love. They commit this mistake by drawing a circle around all of their beliefs and declaring that all of them are fundamental.

Suddenly your church has an official Bible translation, a biblical opinion on mustaches, or an official position on complicated theology about end times. Sometimes these values aren't officially printed in a statement of faith but are nonetheless clear. We believe that the

Holy Spirit needs nine songs and thirty minutes of altar ministry in order to move, or we believe that anyone who doesn't join a particular political party is compromised. And this leads to our third problem.

3. Hedge making causes your church to become elitist. If you remember the story of the Transfiguration (Matt. 17), Peter was up on a mountain praying with Jesus. Suddenly, Moses and Elijah, the two most revered heroes of Jesus' day, appeared and started talking with Christ. In amazement, Peter decides to build shrines to all three of them, when the voice of God suddenly thundered: "This is my Son, whom I love. . . . Listen to him!" (v. 5).

Keep in mind, the majority of hedges in Jesus' day stemmed from Moses and Elijah. God knew that the Pharisees were already incapable of accepting Jesus because He did not value their Mosaic interpretations to the same degree. Indeed, even after this experience, Peter still almost missed God numerous times because of his overcommitment to a Mosaic identity (Gal. 2:11; Acts 11:8). God knew the temple system of Jerusalem would soon be destroyed. He knew that their Jewish traditions, like circumcision, could become a massive hindrance in fulfilling the Great Commission. So, we can understand why God was so dramatic in keeping their focus on Christ alone. Their self-made Jewish identities and their prolific applications of the Law often became their biggest obstacles to future obedience (Acts 15; Phil. 3:5–7; Col. 2:4–12).

Likewise today, there are many people who are Calvinists more than Christians, Charismatics more than followers of Christ. Quite often we use these additional descriptors like shrines unto our theological hedges and heroes. We may not build shrines to Moses or Elijah anymore; but today, we are too often Lutherans, Baptists, Emergents, or [Fill in the Blank], when a simple "child of God" would suffice.

I once visited a church that had a statement of faith that was over twenty pages long! I suggested that they should retitle it, *Why We Are the Only Christians on Planet Earth Going to Heaven.* (They didn't laugh.) I was serious. Not surprisingly, this church had a reputation of ripping on other churches.

In their defense, like many aging churches and movements, they wanted to preserve their theological traditions. Much like the apostle Peter, the motive for hedge making or shrine building is usually good. But there's a dark side to this behavior. The more your church finds its identity in its speculations as opposed to its fundamentals, the more isolated it becomes. It quietly severs unity with the greater body of Christ. It silently expands the definition of a true Christian. Certainly, it seems to reassure us that we're walking the narrow path. But when God routinely breaks out of these boxes, like when He became a Savior to the Gentiles, such hedges ironically cause true obedience to feel like compromise.

> *The more your church finds its identity in its speculations as opposed to its fundamentals, the more isolated it becomes.*

4. Hedge making causes churches to become a hostile place for skeptics or new believers. When a church becomes dominated by a long list of acceptable beliefs, it becomes a threatening place for people to work through skepticism. If a person gives his life to Christ in a highly hedged community, he has a shorter period of time in which he can safely question things. After the grace period has worn off, skepticism is immediately viewed as a threat to the cheap unity that was created through uniformity, not love. The new believer must either put his struggles in the closet (and become indoctrinated) or risk his continued acceptance in order to actually understand his convictions.

But healthy churches are a lot like healthy marriages. Smart people realize that you don't need to see eye to eye in order to walk hand in hand. Biblical unity is not a by-product of thinking alike, but of thinking *together*. Yet, because Christians fail to realize this distinction, we discover the final consequence of hedge making.

> *Biblical unity is not a by-product of thinking alike, but of thinking together.*

5. Church becomes the ultimate distraction from God's mission.
When I first moved to Minneapolis, I was a bit horrified by the quantity of Christians enraptured in academic debates. What disturbed me the most was the fact that Christianity is dying amazingly fast all throughout the city. As I said earlier, only 5.1 percent of our county goes to any evangelical or charismatic church, and the vast majority are senior citizens. Furthermore, of the 5.1 percent that bother to go to church, how many of them even consistently read their Bibles? Frankly, half of the Christians I know aren't mature enough to grasp half of these debates. And it's easy for Christians to forget the fact that American Christianity is a sinking ship. If we can't get lost souls to enter our churches—imperfect as they might be—the whole debate is useless anyway.

This is a microcosm of what's going on in the greater Western church. Evangelical groups are constantly being hijacked by leaders who are obsessed with their hedges and theological shrines. These well-meaning leaders say things like, "If only we all embraced these church formats . . . embraced these inferences, speculations, and opinions . . . THEN we'd experience revival." Of course, their goal is to preserve the church by creating uniformity of thought. But what if the real problem is unity of purpose, regardless of opinion?

Remember some of the final prayers of Christ? He prayed that His disciples would be one (John 17:22). Why can't we simply celebrate the amazing number of things we agree upon? Most of us agree: Jesus is Lord. In no other name is there salvation. There is a heaven. There is a hell. And if we give a rip, we need to reach this world.

If approximately 225 million people die every day, that's almost 3 people per second. As I'm writing this, the news just reported that an average of 300 Somali children died of starvation and preventable disease every day over the last six months. More than 2,000 kids die every day of preventable diseases due to poverty. We haven't even gotten the Bible translated into every language yet. I mean, we're failing on some pretty basic issues.

THE ART OF HEDGE MAKING

So when I get to heaven, I don't want to hear Jesus say, "OK, so you let five billion people go to hell just because you couldn't affiliate with the rest of my team on earth who had different ideas—half of whom were actually right?"

If we could simply get 10 percent of evangelicals to give 10 percent of their income to church, we'd have hundreds of millions of excess dollars to solve the largest global problems. Can you imagine if a meager 20 percent actually took this challenge? We'd take over the earth. The question is not whether we have the power to go and make disciples of all nations. The question is: Can we stay in unity and go together?

> *If we could simply get 10 percent of evangelicals to give 10 percent of their income to church, we'd have hundreds of millions of excess dollars to solve the largest global problems.*

I assure you that none of these things will ever happen as long as we fail to keep our faith simple, as Jesus did. There will always be differing opinions. And these differences may, at times, challenge our sense of security. Yet, despite our best intentions to protect people, we may ironically be accomplishing the exact opposite.

Let's fall in love with humility-filled debates. Let's be quick to admit that we might be wrong. And yes, let's continue to defend the fundamentals of Christianity with tenacity. But, without a true spirit of unity and humility, we will not only kill our desire for God's Word, but our legacy will look more like the nameless, faceless Pharisees than the likeness of our Lord.

CHAPTER SIX IN REVIEW

Key Ideas

1. God has a dramatic bias toward Christians who live in unity with other believers.

2. We simply have more power together than when we seek God alone.

3. All human beings have the sinful tendency to take their opinions, inferences, and speculations and pass them off as fundamentals.

4. Hedge making often becomes a substitute for listening to the Holy Spirit or discerning God's will.

5. Hedge making causes people to seek God's Word less.

6. Homogenous groups of Christians seek indoctrination more than Scripture.

7. Hedge making causes the church to become elitist.

8. Hedge making causes churches to become a hostile place for skeptics or newer believers.

9. Biblical unity is not a by-product of thinking alike but rather thinking together.

10. Church becomes the ultimate distraction from God's mission.

Discussion Questions

1. Have you ever seen an undeniable miracle? If so, share it.

2. Why is it easier to create rules than it is to establish principles?

3. Describe a time when you have been subjected to unreasonable hedge making. How did it make you feel?

4. How might Matthew 18:19 change the way you pray?

5. How have you used prayer in an attempt to control God?

6. What were your thoughts on the belief continuum? Have you ever made one of your convictions or speculations out to be more absolute than it is? Or, have you ever changed opinions altogether about certain beliefs? If so, what issues?

7. Did your parents ever make any protective hedges for you? Are there times when protective hedges or rules might be necessary? If so, when and on what issues?

8. What are three biblical principles by which you should live?

9. In what areas of life do you need more biblical protection? With whom can you work on this area of life?

10. Of the following five principles, do any of them stick out to you as particularly troubling? If so, which ones and why?

- Hedge making often becomes a substitute for listening to the Holy Spirit or discerning God's will.
- Hedge making causes people to seek God's Word less.
- Hedge making causes your church to become elitist.
- Hedge making causes churches to become a hostile place for skeptics or newer believers.
- Church becomes the ultimate distraction from God's mission.

The Rise of Rabid Pets (Part I)

If I were to accidentally kill my church, how might I do this?

Have you ever had a pet peeve? (Like slow-merging cars or people who think Facebook is a functional place to confront others?) For instance, I have this amazing ability to get stupid songs stuck in my head. That's why I can't stand *Dora the Explorer* or the music at most health clubs. Somehow, no matter how long I'm at the gym, I end up with the song "Pump Up the Jam" in my head. And then there's no escape for me.

All day long I'm forced to pump and stump the jam, which gets really awkward when I'm trying to write a serious sermon or read the Gospels. I don't even know what it means to pump up the jam. The same song also gets stuck in my head when I'm making peanut butter sandwiches. And, quite mysteriously, my wife immediately knows when it gets stuck in my head. But my point is this: A pet peeve is something that personally drives us nuts, like nose picking, kids' pizza places, or mime evangelism (as if communicating God's love wasn't hard enough).

But in this chapter, we're going to talk about a different kind of personal pet; it's called a *pet purpose*. Everyone's got one. And it has a mammoth effect on how happy your church experience might be.

But before we unpack this peculiar phenomenon, I need to explain a few things that might seem a bit basic.

UNPACKING THE FIVE PURPOSES

Here's a deep question for you: What is a biblical church? We could probably lose ourselves in an endless debate here. In the book *Purpose Driven Church*, Rick Warren eloquently addressed this question by picking five main themes, or purposes, to a biblical church. Of course, he could have easily chosen thirty-two, but to be simple, he focused on: evangelism, fellowship, discipleship, ministry, and worship.

Certainly, it's important to distinguish purposes from methods or formats. For example, there are a lot of ways to do church: contemporary, traditional, megachurch, small church, home church, snake-handling church, etc. There are a lot of methods that I wouldn't recommend. But, no matter how you do church—format or size—the transcendent purposes of a biblical church remains the same.

So, if you want to be a healthy, biblical church, you can't aim for merely one or two of these purposes unless you want to produce a bizarre school of fish. At some point, we all need a more systematic strategy for accomplishing all five. But indulge me as I break this down a little more.

If you attend a biblical church, there will be a successful effort to be evangelistic (Acts 1:8; Phil.1:6; 1 Thess. 2:8). Evangelism is just a fancy word for sharing your faith in a fruitful way. I'm not saying that everyone will respond to your message, but if you're sharing your faith and hardly anyone responds, you may want to reevaluate your method. After all, there are a never-ending number of freakish ways that people evangelize.

I've never been a big fan of Christian bumper stickers. I'm certain there are probably a few people who've completely turned their lives around after reading one. But how do you do nice things in cars? How do we proactively exude happiness and rainbows while we drive? I suppose we could smile and wave at everyone we see or mount a giant plastic unicorn on our roof racks. Unless we regularly throw money out of our windows, I'm just not sure it compensates for the occasional bad merge or green light space-out.

And as I mentioned in the introduction, I've never understood how people can spread the gospel by vandalizing toilet stalls. Nothing pulls in the lost like, "Call God for a good time," or, "Jezuz wuz here . . . prayin.'" Besides, if a person actually responded, you've given them a terrible conversion story: "How did you receive Christ?" . . . "Well, I was sitting on a toilet and . . ." You see, I think we can do better.

Another odd evangelism technique is called *missionary dating* or, as I prefer, *loveangelism*. It's when you date people into the body of Christ. The only problem is, once you break up with them (so you can win your next convert), they have a tendency to stop going to church. Besides, it always gets a bit awkward when God "anoints you" to reach more than one at the same time.

Then there's the classic gospel-tract-disguised-as-a-twenty-dollar-bill approach. A restaurant waitress recently told me that she gets these instead of tips all the time. After all, nothing says, "God Loves You" like a fake and deceptive blessing. I mean, imagine if God returned the technique on us when we enter heaven, "Surprise! You thought you were saved? Psych! Boy did I sucker you!" In the end deception, vandalism, and lust don't marry well with evangelism.

Evangelism methods vary from street witnessing to social justice outreach to the poor (Acts 3:6). Other Christians will apply this purpose via evangelistic church services (aka attractional churches). We can endlessly debate the pros and cons, but the point is that no matter how you apply evangelism, a biblical church is going to work hard at reaching the lost unless it's disconnected from Christ and His power (John 15; Matt. 28:19).

A biblical church is also going to be passionate about fellowship. Church isn't about getting people to attend a church service. It's a family (1 Thess. 2:8; Gal. 6:2; Heb. 10:24–25; Acts 2:42). As we mentioned earlier in this book, intimate Christian friends are one of the single greatest statistical predictors of spiritual growth. Thus, it's foolish to think we can disciple people without first providing a

Bible-based family they can do life with. We all need intimate accountability and encouragement, which is the heartbeat of biblical fellowship (1 Cor. 15:33; Heb. 3:13; 10:24–25).

Ministry and serving others are divine distractions that free us from the tyranny of our overly magnified needs.

In addition to evangelism and fellowship, a biblical church is going to provide every member with ministry opportunities. God created us to do good works (Eph. 2:10). Indeed, ministry is one of the quickest ways we can spiritually refresh ourselves (Prov. 11:25; Acts 20:35). In fact, next to fellowship, numerous studies have shown that ministry involvement is also one of the top statistical predictors of spiritual growth.[41] We can attempt to help everyone solve their problems, or we can give them something that's simply bigger than their problems. Ministry and serving others are divine distractions that free us from the tyranny of our overly magnified needs. Thus, once these foundational purposes fall in place, churches can then effectively participate in what I like to call the deeper disciplines: discipleship and worship.

Discipleship is often characterized as learning Bible doctrines. But it's far more than the acquisition of information. Rather, it's the adaptation of a biblical lifestyle. In other words, do our sexuality, our time, our money, and our thoughts conform to the likeness of Christ? Would Christ *loveangelize*?

And the biblical purpose of worship doesn't merely speak to how emotional we get in church services. Worship is a lifestyle of communicating with our heavenly Father. In other words, how much time do we spend in intercession throughout the day? Do we ever slow down enough to listen for the prophetic voice of God in our hearts? Do we live a lifestyle of thankfulness? Do we use our finances, words, and emotions as tools of praise to our creator? You see, a biblical church can't merely specialize in just one of these areas. At some point, our desire for health will demand that we advocate for all of these things.

WHAT IS YOUR PET PURPOSE?

But here is where things get stimulating. Every Christian has a favorite church experience—one that stirs up their passion for God more than the others. Thus, one of the first things we do when new people join our church community is help them identify their pet purpose, which is one of the five biblical purposes that personally charges them up the most.

For example, at one time, my pet purpose used to be worship and prayer. It was all I was interested in. I rarely went a day without praying for an hour or two. Not surprisingly, I also wanted my church to provide endless worship experiences for me. It was so new and refreshing. Sunday-morning worship experiences were never good enough. I could happily attend worship services two or three hours at a time. But surprisingly, this pet purpose actually changed for me.

In another season of my life, all I wanted was discipleship. I memorized amazing quantities of Scripture with other people. I read systematic theology like it was the most entertaining topic on planet earth. I couldn't get enough. And during this season I would have been quite content attending a church that exclusively did two-hour expository messages on Leviticus.

And you may not get as obsessive as I do, but everyone has a pet purpose. It's not a bad thing. It's just a function of the body of Christ that specifically inspires you. And for some of you it might be due to your calling. God has gifted you in some very specific ways (Eph. 4:11). Other times, God is simply moving in our lives in a specific way; thus, we simply prefer one of the five more than the others. But here's where things get dysfunctional.

A lot of times Christians (or churches) get so overcommitted to their pet purpose that they start to define it as more spiritual than

> *A lot of times Christians (or churches) get so overcommitted to their pet purpose that they start to define it as more spiritual than others.*

others. Have you experienced this yet? They often say, "If you were really connected to Christ, then you'd do all prophetic worship all the time." "If this were really a 'biblical church,' then you'd primarily give your lives to . . . social justice . . . end-times theology . . . prayer, etc." Sometimes it's a purpose. Sometimes it's a pet theology.

Everyone is passionate about his or her pet purpose. But many Christians start to say things like, "If you don't value my pet purpose above all, then you're compromised." In fact, whenever the word *compromise* is used in Christian debates, it's incredibly common to be coming from someone who is overcommitted to their pet purpose.

I like to call this a *rabid* pet purpose—Christians start foaming at the mouth until everyone agrees with their narrow idea of church. Quite often they declare that a biblical church is one that showcases their favorite pet purpose on Sunday mornings. If the rabid pet purpose is two hours of prophetic worship, then any primary church service without this is compromised. If the rabid pet purpose is discipleship and the local pastor isn't meaty enough, then the church is watered down. After all, their beloved pet has become an elite breed that needs special food. It's the only breed that makes God cry tears of joy whenever a church embraces its furry wonder. Thus, these rabid pets go around and bite everyone else's pet into submission.

When Jesus referred to rabid pets, He preferred the term *wolves* (Matt. 7:15–16; 10:16–17). And Jesus generally reserved this term for describing deeply religious people. As I discussed in chapter five, most of the people who destroy the body of Christ do so under the pretense of protecting it. The great irony is that most wolves see themselves as super sheep.

Hence, these diseased people no longer pick a church based on how fruitful or balanced the community is. They no longer pick a church based on how much it will stretch them or their family. Rather, they expect their pet purpose to get snuggled on Sunday morning and

> *Most of the people who destroy the body of Christ do so under the pretense of protecting it.*

get upset when the pastor or budget committee doesn't fund their pet project. When they advocate for their pet, these people never see it as a self-centered thing; it's always presented as the most utilitarian or best choice for the body of Christ. And rabid pets generally manifest themselves around debates about worship formats, message formats, or anything pertaining to church methodology.

PUTTING A LEASH ON YOUR PET

Truth be told, rabid pets come in every shape and size. They don't just come from *Charismania Kate* or *Calvinazi Joe*. They take a hold of every age and ethnicity. I've had friends go to conferences and come back rabid. I've noticed that certain churches and books tend to transmit spiritual rabies more than others. But rather than point fingers, let's look to see if we might have rabid pet purposes of our own that are growling away in our hearts.

So here is an introspective question for you: What does a *deep* church look like? Or what is a *deep* sermon? Your answers to these questions often reveal your pet purpose or theology. And again, it's not wrong to have a pet purpose—as long as you know when to put a leash on your pet. But what does a leash look like?

At our church, a leash on your pet means that you don't need Sunday morning church services to be all about your purpose. No Christians should assume that their church's main services are de-signed for them. There are many potential audiences that your pastor has in mind. Like a busy emergency room, pastors constantly have to make complicated decisions about who should receive the most at-tention. So don't assume that it's you, especially if you're a long-term Christian and you know how to feed yourself.

Even more, in a healthy church, services should only be a small slice of a weekly church experience. It's impossible to meet ev-eryone's needs in a singular service. And really, this is the same thing Paul talked about in Romans 14:20 when he said, "Do not destroy the work of God for the sake of [your personal issue]." Or, to the Corinthians, he said, "Each one of you has a hymn, or a word of instruction, a revelation, a tongue or an interpretation" (1 Cor. 14:26). Some want hymns, others want teaching, still others want prophecy. And some of these experiences freak people out (v. 23). Of course, Paul wasn't forbidding them; rather, he was simply saying to put a leash on it. There's a proper time and place for everything. But don't think you're more spiritual (v. 36). And don't you dare disunite the church body over these kinds of debates (12:21) unless you're a hyperspiritual baby (13:11).

> *They're immature spiritual babies who quote scriptures and rip on other churches until everyone coddles their pet ideas and preferences. Entire denominations are embroiled in debates over pet purposes while Christianity slides toward total obsolescence.*

Unfortunately, that's a perfect description of a lot of long-term Christians. They're immature spiritual babies who quote scriptures and rip on other churches until everyone coddles their pet ideas and preferences. Entire denominations are embroiled in debates over pet purposes while Christianity slides toward total obsolescence.

FOAMING AT THE MOUTH

A while back I had a church leader come to me with a serious concern. At the time, I was totally overwhelmed by our church. We had literally grown by close to four hundred members that month alone, at least half of whom had no previous church experience.

That week was particularly overwhelming because three of our brand-new attendees had made suicide attempts, and I was the only person they felt comfortable calling. That same week I also had more than a dozen people confess a sex addiction to me, not to mention the two gentlemen who asked me to help them beat their meth addiction. The needs of our church felt so overwhelming. So I wasn't exactly excited to meet with this long-time church member, but since she was a leader, I freed up my schedule.

As soon as I saw her face, I knew something was wrong. She looked pretty upset. So I immediately popped the cork, "What's up?" Her first words were, "This church doesn't give a rip about outreach. I'm sick and tired of it! And I'm not sure I can stay here any longer." Of course, I was totally shocked. Our entire church was like an orphanage that was overwhelmed by abandoned kids. I felt as though I was holding a dozen babies in my hands listening to someone rant about how I didn't care about babies. It seemed ludicrous.

I finally asked her, "What does *outreach* mean to you?" Of course, she had just read a book by a rabid Christian that claimed missional communities to multiethnic homeless people are the ultimate form of outreach. She didn't merely have a pet purpose for evangelism; she had a pet methodology. She obviously resented the fact that our church was so good at attractional church methods. And it was clear that she didn't want to judge me or our church by our fruit. Rather, like many diseased Christians, she began to judge according to format as well.

Of course, like a lot of pastors, a part of me wanted to indulge her and promise to start a soup kitchen ministry for her. After all, I deeply believe in these types of ministries, and I loved this leader. Yet, it was painfully clear, our church had bigger fish to fry. The only reason we hadn't started a ministry like that already was because we didn't have any leaders or resources to do so. And I knew that I'd literally die if I tried to launch any more ministries at that time.

And don't get me wrong; I love social justice and am an advocate for racial reconciliation. Sadly, this leader didn't hang around very long. And it's especas a knowledge tially sad knowing that, only a few months later, we ended up launching dozens of amazing ministries that were right up her alley. But, like a lot of people who get rabid pets, they lose their ability to discern the greater will of God. As a result, these impatient Christians become revival seekers rather than revival makers. Instead of being joyfully contagious, they become cynically contentious. And in the process, the church loses the ultimate catalyst for growth: unity.

To amplify this problem, we're seeing the rise of an unprecedented number of parachurch ministries—ministries that operate outside the confines of the local church (e.g., pro-life organizations, missions, social justice organizations, houses of prayer, etc.). Ironically, many of these organizations were formed because they no longer fit within the political confines of a local church or denomination (often a church with a rabid-pet problem). Yet, by design, parachurch organizations are often devoted to a singular pet purpose.

If parachurch organizations aren't constantly championing the local church (warts and all), they often become incubators of idealism and rabidness that cause their followers to become Bride haters—people who are so opinionated about church that they functionally become incompatible with God's local church.

The problem, however, is that many of their followers, who often have a weak connection with a healthy congregation, end up getting an extremely narrow approach to Christianity. The organization isn't a church; therefore, it can selectively apply a niche number of biblical mandates. If parachurch organizations aren't constantly championing the local church (warts and all), they often become incubators of idealism and rabidness that cause their followers to become Bride haters—people who are so opinionated about church that they functionally become incompatible with God's local church.

Honestly, it really disturbs me that many of the top Christian authors that young people are reading aren't successful practicing pastors. I realize there are many brilliant nonpastors that all of us should be reading. However, there's an amazing number of Christians who are deconstructing church without any impressive experience in reconstructing it. Despite the increase in bizarre new approaches to church, many of these new models aren't actually more effective in reaching the unchurched. Hence, the few young people who still remain in our churches are being accosted with idealism and rabid pets the size of King Kong. It's no wonder so many people are abandoning the church.

> *There's an amazing number of Christians who are deconstructing church without any impressive experience in reconstructing it.*

PREYING UPON THE OLD AND SMALL

Eventually, churches can become dominated by someone's rabid pet. Indeed, entire denominations can fall prostrate to such pets. Of course, the smaller or older a church gets, the easier this becomes. Here's why.

In smaller churches, the economic fabric of the church usually comes down to a small number of family clans. When one of them becomes rabid, it becomes difficult for the church to cut them loose because the church is often economically and relationally codependent with them. That's why I always tell pastors of smaller churches to get extra margin in their budgets. And why?

Church leaders are inundated with dozens of subjective decisions. Just about every year there comes a complicated decision that will cost you about two to five families. In fact, if your church's decisions aren't costing you followers from time to time, you probably aren't following Christ (John 6:66). Rabid families will immediately hate the change, no matter what it is. And the remaining four families are the sympathizer families that can't understand why you rudely won't snuggle their crazy dog any longer. Thus, if you can't financially afford to lose all five families, then you'll be stuck with a slowly sinking ship—making political decisions rather than healthy decisions.[42]

In older churches, there's usually a different reason why rabid pets take over. Most churches in America go into a permanent plateau after about fifteen to eighteen years.[43] There are a lot of reasons this happens (and, as we'll see in

Quite commonly, churches also tend to stop growing after their founding pastor resigns.

upcoming chapters, there are a lot of remedies). Quite commonly, churches also tend to stop growing after their founding pastor resigns. Thus, it's important to ask why this is a lethal turning point for most churches.

When most founding pastors leave, many churches fall into a never-ending power-vacuum. Even if someone fills the pulpit well, very few fill the political shoes well. Thus the church becomes a huge fight amidst staff or power families over rabid pet purposes. Of course, not all dogfights happen in the open air. They happen in board meetings, staff meetings, or any place where Christians share their concerns (aka criticisms) without a clear view of the big picture. Yet, very few people have enough clout to reconsolidate power and reunify people after the founding pastor leaves, unless they simply outlast everyone else.

Thus, most aging churches stay in a constant yet quiet civil war. Rather than being called to the "central leader," people's allegiances shift to being called to the house or the gangs of rabid pets that huddle around a specific ministry.

Subsequent pastors live in a constant state of political pet snuggling. Indeed, most pastors who succeed the founder win the position through pet snuggling more than decisive leadership. And whoever has the most dominant pet usually controls the tradition that all leaders must subsequently give homage to.

Many of you grew up in these kinds of churches. That's why you've given up on church as a functional institution. But the good news is, it doesn't have to be this way. Despite being bitten by many well-meaning pets over the years, I still believe that church can be the most refreshing place on earth.

But how do we deal with rabid pets? What if we're sick and tired of leashing our pets? What if the pastor is dysfunctional and preventing health, which is why our pets are becoming rabid in the first place? Well, get ready. We're going to hit all of these questions and more in the next chapter.

CHAPTER SEVEN IN REVIEW

Key Ideas

1. No matter how you do church, the transcendent purposes of a biblical church remain the same.

2. A biblical church is going to work hard at reaching the lost unless it's disconnected from Christ and His power.

3. A biblical church is also going to be passionate about fellowship.

4. A biblical church is going to provide every member with ministry opportunities.

5. Ministry and serving others are divine distractions that free us from the tyranny of our overly magnified needs.

6. Discipleship is the adaptation of a biblical lifestyle.

7. In a healthy church, services should only be a small slice of a weekly church experience.

8. There's an amazing number of Christians who are deconstructing church without any interest in reconstructing it.

9. Most churches in America go into a permanent plateau after about fifteen to eighteen years.

10. Churches tend to stop growing after their founding pastor resigns.

Discussion Questions

1. Have you ever experienced a strange form of evangelism? What was it? And how did it make you feel?

2. What do you think is the purpose of your church? Why do you attend?

3. Which of the five biblical purposes do you tend to focus on the least: evangelism, fellowship, discipleship, ministry, or worship? Or which of these five could you stand to grow in the most? Why?

4. What should your church expect from you? Are you meeting its expectations?

5. How is your purpose for being in your church influenced by your spiritual gifts?

6. What is your pet purpose? What is a deep church to you?

7. Is it the church's job to facilitate your spiritual growth? Why or why not?

8. Has your pet purpose ever changed? How did it change?

9. In your opinion, what do you think the difference is between a pet purpose and a rabid pet purpose?

10. Describe the kind of church you would like to see established.

Preventing Dogfights (Rabid Pets, Part II)

How do we circumvent complicated church debates and deficiencies?

Eating healthy has become tricky. There are dozens of types of eaters: vegetarians, vegans, and organic naturalists. But rather than being a health-food junkie, I consider myself to be "junk-food healthy." It's a name I created for a special breed of people like myself who try to stay healthy while primarily eating junk food. And, yes, it occasionally feels odd (like when you swig down your vitamins with a soda), but I meticulously maintain a healthy weight. I may not be able to make my pectorals dance anymore, but they also don't shimmy rebelliously when I do the Macarena.

It is true that I love organic foods, especially when I wrap them around a Twinkie. I think we all need to watch where our food comes from as well as be aware of health food marketing gimmicks. I was looking at the package of a snack cake the other day. It literally claimed to be a good source of Vitamin C, as though this somehow compensated for the giant blockage it was about to create in my arteries. For even more comfort, the company boldly claimed that this treat was only twenty calories per serving. But, a careful look revealed that each cake was ten servings, which would be perfect if we were a village of happily singing Smurfs.

But even health-food junkies would admit there is no single food that can meet all of our dietary needs. Even more, there is no way to stay healthy if you only eat one meal every seven days. So then, why do so many Christians act as though a single church service could meet all of their spiritual needs?

Even more, no matter what kind of worship you have, it's either going to be too long, too short, too seeker-friendly, too charismatic, too liturgical, or too progressive for somebody. Unfortunately, dysfunctional churches usually respond by taking one of three cancerous paths:

1. Leaders start creating services that cater to their noisiest long-time attendees as opposed to the people the church needs to reach the most.

2. Many churches simply blend five styles of worship into a putrid stew that nobody ends up liking. Grandpa finally decides to rap in church worship with his brand-new, comb-over fauxhawk, and neither the seniors nor the youth end up liking it.

3. Leaders simply start saying, "We just don't do that here." Hence they lock everyone's good-natured pets in the closet just because a few rabid pets drove everyone nuts.

As the pastor of a sizable church, I can empathize with this third response more than any of the others. I'm constantly being pressured by people to launch ministries that go outside of our organization's gift-mix or resources. And sometimes leaders need to make difficult decisions about timing. Much like a fifteen-year-old girl shouldn't have a baby, some churches simply aren't ready to birth certain ministries.

However, many pastors are chopping off biblical purposes from their churches, not realizing that God created these things for our overall health. For example, a pastor friend of mine once said, "We simply don't do small groups." Unfortunately, he thought he was wisely clarifying the vision for his church. As a good friend (and an obsessive researcher of church health), I told him in a nonoppressive way that small groups are one of the greatest statistical predictors of both church growth and church health.[44] Even more, the statistical odds of church splits and disgruntlement is dramatically higher in churches without strong small groups.[45]

> *Ironically, many of the rabid pets that bite pastors are inadvertently created by pastors who were convinced they needed a narrow vision of church to achieve success.*

There are a few flaws to the simple-is-always-smarter approach to church. We can't merely neglect certain things and then live in a fantasy world of pretend church health, even though it makes the political reality of our churches easier. Eventually such churches will experience the following symptoms: they will implode into a pile of unbalanced weirdness; they will fail to produce long-term transformation due to an anemic diet; or they'll end up alienating a larger number of people that could have easily been empowered with a different way of thinking.

You can't simply lock a healthy dog in a closet and expect it to stay happy. Ironically, many of the rabid pets that bite pastors are inadvertently created *by* pastors who were convinced they needed a narrow vision of church to achieve success. Yet, ultimately we've got to have a place where *all five* of the purposes of a biblical church can be manifested.

So how do we accomplish this? I suggest three powerful solutions that will keep you and your church free from the above problems. Here is how we can keep our churches a happy yet effective place. And the first solution stays in line with our ridiculous rabid dog analogy.

HEALTHY CHURCHES CREATE DOG PARKS

I might not be able to snuggle everyone's pet on Sunday morning, but I don't have to lock everyone's pet in the closet to deal with them. Instead, we create a place in our church where everyone's pet can run around with an appropriate amount of freedom. This, however, is next to impossible without a sophisticated small-group system.

At Substance, we've intentionally designed an amazing number of church models and experiences under one roof. We have weekend church experiences that range from a few hundred into the thousands. So *you can choose* your favorite church size. If you want home churches, we've got them. If you want deep experiential worship and altar ministry, we have midweek services that last for hours on end. Besides, in a healthy church, services should only be a small slice of a holistic discipleship experience. Most mature Christians know this; hence, they don't even participate in silly formatting debates.

We are, by no means, a church that has everything. Despite our spiritual buffet, there are still people who get frustrated because they can't special order something else. We never start a ministry without a passionate and qualified leader (a combination that is sometimes quite rare). And not every program is able to be staff-led or church-funded. But whenever we become aware of a legitimate missing need in our church, there's a powerful biblical pattern of provision that every Christian must follow. So let's read about how the apostles created dog parks in the early church.

THE CHURCH'S FIRST DOG PARK

In Acts 6, we read of a social justice–oriented problem. Widows were being overlooked in the distribution of food. Thus, good-natured pet purposes came barking at the apostles front door. But the apostles said, "It would not be right for us to neglect the ministry of the word of God in order to wait on tables" (Acts 6:2). In other words, we're not going to change our sense of calling, even for a legitimate spiritual or physical need. We have a clear obligation before God. Yet, despite this firm stance, they also didn't lock these good-natured pups in the closet either. So listen to their solution, "Brothers, [you] choose seven men from among you who are known to be full of the Spirit and wisdom. We will turn this responsibility over to them and will give our attention to prayer and the ministry of the word" (vv. 3–4).

In other words, the apostles didn't actually take on new responsibilities, nor did they denounce that it was a legitimate need. This could have exploded into a massive dogfight. Scripture could have been used as a weapon. This could have

> *Instead of dogfighting and Scripture thrashing, the people courageously honored the wishes of the apostles.*

become the first church split. But watch what happens. Scripture gives us a stellar example of organizational maturity.

Instead of dogfighting and Scripture thrashing, the people courageously honored the wishes of the apostles. Picking the seven probably took a lot more time than we'd like to imagine. Someone had to make difficult decisions before the top seven leaders were found. People could have whined, "I don't want seven new leaders! I love it when the apostle Peter comes by my table! Nobody does it like him." But instead they honored the apostles' ability to discern God's will.

And because everyone responded with maturity, patience, and honor, God ended up sending them a revival of sorts. Verse seven says that "the number of disciples in Jerusalem increased rapidly, and a large number of priests became obedient to the faith."

Notice that God sent them more leaders (aka priests), which is God's reward for organizational maturity. Adding leaders is something that every organization is looking to do. The apostles didn't cave in and take on a responsibility that God wasn't calling them to, and the people didn't whine about having to do a search process that fit with the apostles' criteria. The results speak for themselves: God not only sent a revival, but He sent them more leaders.

> *Immature followers demand pastoral energy or funding because they don't want the burden of being resourceful, and the result is leaders leave these churches faster than ever.*

Unfortunately, the exact opposite process happens in most churches. When churches become a battleground of rabid pets, many immature leaders simply lock up the pets, "We don't do that here." Immature followers demand pastoral energy or funding because they don't want the burden of being resourceful, and the result is leaders leave these churches faster than ever. And where are they going? They probably transfer to churches that have a healthier and more patient approach to creating dog parks. After all, who wants to serve amidst a faithless group of adult babies? Not me.

But going beyond dog parks, how else might we prevent dog-fights? Part of the solution rests in redefining people's entire concept of church, which leads us to our second solution.

HEALTHY CHURCHES AVOID CHURCH SERVICE CHRISTIANITY

As I said earlier, it's impossible to meet everyone's needs and desires in a singular service (unless it's five hours long). Even then, it's impossible to adequately reach every audience (seekers, newbies, and goldie-oldies). And, in some ways, this entire debate reveals a narrow concept of church.

A while back, I had a man come up to me after my message. I had just finished praying with a group of people who gave their lives to Christ. It was a powerful moment. Yet the look on this man's face was a stark contrast to those of the new believers I had been talking with.

He jumped right in with a bold conclusion, "I can tell this isn't a Bible-believing church." A bit stunned by his bluntness, I asked, "How so?" He began, "Well, you only shared about nine Bible verses in your message." And then he ranted about all the "fluff and filler" I had in my message.

In my mind I started asking, *What would have been the magical number of scriptures? Would heaven open up if I shared ten Bible verses? Did I miss the anointing quota?* But he continued blasting me about how I should exclusively preach expository messages—that is, line-by-line preaching through Scripture.

I have to admit: I love my fluff. I'm darn proud of my fluff. If I can make a person laugh or engage them through good storytelling, then I can share increasingly difficult truths. As the theologian Mary

Poppins once said, "A spoonful of sugar helps the medicine go down." Believe it or not, this is actually a scientific phenomenon.

Recently, there was a study done on the science of persuasion. Scientists have long noted that when we hold an extended conversation with others, our heart rates and breathing actually syncs up. Studies show that this physiological phenomenon, often called entrainment, usually precedes persuasion.[46]

In other words, it's hard to persuade people (i.e., evangelize or disciple them) before this phenomenon occurs. And take a wild guess what is the fastest way to create entertainment . . . laughter. Humor is one of the most potent ingredients to persuasion on earth. In fact, one of the largest church health studies found that laughter in a church is actually a statistical predictor of both health and growth![47] So, in your face, Mr. Fluffhead. (Perhaps I'm still a bit wounded?)

After Mr. Fluffhead finished his spiritual judgment, he paused to see what I would do, perhaps hoping I would tearfully repent and become more religious like him. And don't get me wrong, I love expository preaching. But if transformation was entirely about God's written Word, then we should exclusively do Bible recitations with absolutely no commentary whatsoever (and in Greek and Hebrew, of course). Based on this man's criteria, Jesus wouldn't have been considered Bible-believing either. Sometimes Jesus or Paul would preach an entire message without quoting a single scripture, and it's not like they didn't have the text available to them.

And to be fair, this man also misunderstood the primary target audience of my message. He assumed our church services are for Christians—or people like him who already believe in the Bible.

So I finally said, "Sir, it's interesting to me that you can tell if I'm Bible-believing by listening to a single message. You see, here at Substance, we believe that Bible-believing is a lifestyle—not a church service or a sermon format. And if you really wanted to know if I was Bible-believing, you'd have to spend the week with me.

"And if you did, you would have seen me memorizing a Bible passage this morning with my three kids. If you did, you would have seen me do my morning devotions. If you did, you would have seen my wife and I pray together. And you would have seen my staff and I speak to one another in psalms, hymns, and spiritual songs." I was just setting him up for my climax . . .

But a healthy church is like a healthy diet; we need numerous feeding opportunities throughout the week that are designed for numerous needs.

"It seems apparent to me that you think Christianity is a church service. And you probably think the gospel is a mere message. But here, we don't even see this service as church. And the last thing I'm gonna do is jam a big chunk of biblical meat down a spiritual baby's throat just so that I can appease a big baby Christian like you." (I didn't actually say that last statement. But, man, it would have been a great zinger.) As I said this, I imagined Jesus alley-ooping the ball to me as I did a reverse slam dunk.

At first, Mr. Fluffhead didn't know how to respond. I could tell that my response flew right over his head. As we continued to talk, it was apparent that he had a disease I call "Church Service Christianity." It's when Christians start to think that the Sunday service actually *is* the church.

People with this disease think that the Sunday service needs to be the total summation of a church's gospel. That's why they fatally assume they can know a church by attending its church service. But a healthy church is like a healthy diet; we need numerous feeding opportunities throughout the week that are designed for numerous needs.

That's why we regularly tell our congregation, "Church doesn't start until the service is over." Indeed, "Church is what happens in between church services." Church is a lifestyle of accountability, not a church-service format. Bible-believing is a lifestyle of Bible application not a sermon format. Charismatic is a lifestyle of trusting

Church is a lifestyle of accountability, not a church-service format.

for the miraculous, not a worship format. I've noticed that impoverished and persecuted Christians seem to understand this distinction far better than wealthy Westerners. After all, their circumstances tend to prevent them from idolatrously confusing such formats for the real thing.

So, aside from parroting a few catchphrases, how do we help Christians redefine the purpose of church? One suggestion came from a wise mentor of mine named Billy Hornsby.

Billy once told me about his visit to a Rolls Royce dealership in England. Being an extreme luxury vehicle for the super wealthy, the Rolls Royce showroom floor was absolutely spectacular. The whole area made you feel as though you were the most important person in the world.

As my friend sat down inside this brilliant machine, the aroma of supple leather wafted up. The dashboard shimmered. It was glorious. And as the door closed, it was like heaven itself had enveloped him. So, putting both hands on the steering wheel, my normally frugal friend started thinking, *This car would certainly change my life.*

Of course, he could never justify spending the money. Besides, everything loses its shine with time. Yet, the whole experience was so sensational, it ended up becoming one of the highlights of his trip.[48]

I listened to Billy tell his story like an enraptured school kid. But then he started asking me a series of profound questions. "Peter," he said, "have you ever seen a great dealership change the oil on the showroom floor? Probably not. And that's because the showroom floor has one purpose: Help the customer realize, 'I must have this car.'" Then he profoundly added, "Most churches do not have a showroom floor."

Now, if a dealership refused to change the oil in the showroom, no one would assume that they don't believe in oil changes. After all, everyone knows that changing the oil in your vehicle is essential. And that's also why most dealerships have a mechanic shop and a parts department. You want to keep the grease in the back.

Quite simply: immature Christians fail to understand that, just like car dealerships, the maintenance of our souls require numerous departments. We need weekend church services (deemed the showroom floor in many churches). But, we also need small groups or midweek experiences (a mechanic shop or parts department) where we can confess sins or get accountability for specialized issues, the messy stuff. After all, sister So-and-So doesn't want people watching when she gets demonically delivered of snack cakes for the eighth time.

But here's the opposite problem for some churches: They've exclusively become a showroom floor. They have no depth, no dog parks, no mechanic shop. Their narrow vision assumes church members know how to outsource such needs. And if you happen to live in a Bible Belt city or Christian oasis that's replete with discipleship opportunities, more power to you. But most churches around the world would be making a grave mistake by emulating such selectivity.

On the other hand, many churches are exclusively greasy-gross mechanic shops. They've got the deepest discipleship and worship around; yet, the church never really grows—except by transfer growth. To excuse this, they often make up silly excuses like, "We don't have quantity, but we have quality." But over time, churches like these usually lose both.

So to summarize: Every church needs to clarify where they will put their showroom and their mechanic shop. Because, wherever there is ambiguity, rabid dogs will continue to bite.

HEALTHY CHURCHES CREATE AN OTHERS-ORIENTED CULTURE

Finally, at Substance we always tell people, "Nobody gets what they want on Sunday mornings except the one lost sheep that heaven wants to rejoice over." You are certainly free to practice church differently. For us, statements like these not only clarify our showroom floor but they reorient our long-term members from being consumers to servants.

Instead of making our weekend services a self-centered feeding experience, we train our members to think completely differently about church services. To make this applicable, let's say you have four hundred people coming to your church on Sunday. Imagine if one hundred of them came with the exclusive goal of giving someone else a hundred dollars. Who wouldn't want to attend this church?

My wife and I love to practice this type of generosity. Beyond our tithes and offerings, we love to surprise people by paying their monthly mortgages, helping them in crisis, or taking away their oppressive bills. It's not uncommon for us to personally spend an extra five hundred dollars a month on spontaneous benevolence. And if only 25 percent of your four hundred–member church did this, it would add up to a surplus of fifty thousand dollars a month to simply help people who are struggling. Can you imagine what would happen if this much extra benevolence flowed through a church of only four hundred members?

Yet, imagine if another one hundred members came with the exclusive goal of finding someone to encourage, pray for, or fast over all week long. Finally, imagine if another hundred came with the exclusive goal of finding needs to serve. You need a free babysitter this week? . . . Your car needs repairs? . . . Your home needs improvement? No problem. There's a hundred people looking for ways to serve. And finally, imagine that the remaining 25 percent are either unchurched visitors or baby Christians who simply haven't yet become others-oriented in their spirituality.

Can you imagine how amazing this church would be? I mean, three-quarters of the church isn't even coming for themselves whatsoever. Quite simply, this would be a church in revival—a church like Acts 2, which was obsessed with giving, not receiving.

In contrast to this, many long-term Christians still act like infants, as if church was all about them. They act as though they're totally unable to feed themselves or start their own dog parks—a sign of complete immaturity. Hence they pick a church based on what it can do for them rather than on how much the church stretches them to live for the lost. But it's time we grow beyond this silliness.

> *Many long-term Christians still act like infants, as if church was all about them.*

THE ROAD MAP TO HAPPY DOGS

So, to summarize, healthy churches create dog parks and define church as a multiplicity of spiritual experiences. They don't have do-nothing members who defer responsibility nor dictator pastors who refuse to allow diversity. And lastly, they see services as an outlet for serving the lost—not a spiritual buffet for feeding themselves.

And the coolest part is this: Once a church embraces these approaches, it's amazing how many dynamic leaders will flock to such an environment. Soon, your church will have an answer for every spiritual malady.

But this begins when people stop thinking that their preference for church is the ultimate preference. Besides, you'll soon realize that you need a variety of spiritual meals in different seasons of your life. Eventually, you're going to get sick of spiritual Twinkies or pure meat. That is to say, your obsession with prophetic prayer just might give way to intense Bible study, which just might give way to assisting those in poverty. And when these changes happen, you aren't going to want to leave your church or start a dogfight just to find an alternative.

CHAPTER EIGHT IN REVIEW

Key Ideas

1. Many pastors chop off one or more of five biblical purposes for their churches, not realizing that God demands all of these things for our overall health.

2. In a healthy church, services should only be a small slice of a holistic discipleship experience.

3. Healthy churches create ways to meet people where they are and lead them toward spiritual maturity.

4. Immature followers demand pastoral energy or funding because they don't want the burden of being resourceful.

5. Healthy churches avoid church service–driven Christianity.

6. "Church Service Christianity" is when Christians start to think that the Sunday service actually is the church.

7. Bible-believing is a lifestyle of Bible application, not a sermon format.

8. Healthy churches create an others-oriented church culture.

9. Many long-term Christians act as if church is all about them.

10. Healthy churches don't have do-nothing members who defer responsibility nor dictator pastors who refuse to allow diversity; their leaders and members see church as an outlet for serving the lost—not a spiritual buffet for feeding themselves.

Discussion Questions

1. Have you ever been a part of a church fight over a "ministry hole"? How did your experience compare to the example of Acts 6? Compared to the biblical example, would you recommend a different approach now?

2. How does your present church experience compare to the picture of the church in Acts 2?

3. In the last chapter, you identified your personal pet purpose. How might you create a dog park for that purpose?

4. What other dog parks does your church need to consider?

5. How has this chapter reframed the way you think about the Sunday morning church service?

6. In what ministry should you be serving during the week? What keeps others from joining you in this ministry?

7. How do you feed yourself spiritually throughout the week? And how might it affect your Sunday morning church experience?

8. What are three things you can do to feed yourself spiritually throughout the week?

9. If you came to your church to give, which of the following would be easiest and/or hardest for you: giving of your time in prayer and fasting; giving of your finances; or giving of your time in

service to others? Which of these do you think God is most interested in growing you in? Which form of generosity do you think God desires to stretch you with the most?

10. How can you be more resourceful in meeting the needs of the lost in your community?

CHAPTER NINE

The Great Generation Gap

Why are young Westerners leaving the church in droves?

W<small>HEN</small> <small>OTHER</small> <small>PASTORS</small> <small>COME</small> <small>TO</small> S<small>UBSTANCE</small>, they usually say one of two things, "Wow, you guys are way more youthful than any large church I've seen." Or, "Wow, you guys are not a Bible-belt, transfer-growth kind of church. There are a lot of extremely messed-up people here."

Of course, I never know how to respond to the latter one. It would be kind of weird if we ran a hospital filled with predominantly healthy people. In some ways, that's one of my greatest fears for our church. After all, Christians who aren't regularly exposed to the messy lives of drug addicts, cohabiting couples, and the like lose their ability to see God's purpose for His church. As a result of being cloistered, they usually do one of two things:

1. Cloistered Christians analyze and critique everything. When you're standing in an emergency room that doesn't get much use, you start having debates about little stuff: "Should we really be using this type of operating table?

> *It would be kind of weird if we ran a hospital filled with predominantly healthy people.*

What kinds of scrubs should we allow people to wear?" There are certain conversations you just won't care about when someone is bleeding out on the operating table. But when you're removed from this environment, lesser issues become increasingly important.

2. Cloistered churches become unhealthily self-oriented. When churches plateau for more than a year or two, or when churches grow extremely slowly, there's a greater temptation for long-term members to start obsessing over the question, "What do I like?" Hence, the church culture adapts to those who are already coming rather than those the church needs to reach.

BRIDGING THE HUGE GENERATIONAL GAP

Beyond these classic church foibles, I think there's a bigger problem lurking in Western churches. Young people are leaving church for a lot of reasons. But sometimes we miss some of the most obvious reasons.

Recently, I was nerdishly reading through the 2010 census of the United States. As a huge advocate of church planting, I was hoping to learn a few strategies about how we can better suit our church plants to the needs of our evolving culture. Yet, a few of the stats ended up smacking me right between the eyes.

According to the census, the majority of Americans are now under forty years old. The largest of this group are young twenty-somethings. This, by itself, isn't incredibly unique. Most developing countries are even more youthful than the U.S. However, this is actually quite profound when you consider that the vast majority of American pastors and church decision makers are quickly becoming senior citizens.

To put this another way, there's roughly a two- to three-decade age difference between the majority of church decision makers and the average American. When you think about it, that's a massive cultural disparity, especially when the largest and most receptive unchurched demographic is actually closer to four decades apart from the average American pastor.

When I realized this, my mind started freaking out. I started thinking about all of the worship wars that churches get caught in. I started thinking about all the mean-spirited debates about postmodern Christians. And then I thought, "What if all of these tensions are simply a symptom of a massive generation gap in the church?"

> *But there is also a direct correlation between the median age of a church and its odds of reaching unchurched people.*

Certainly this age disparity must be affecting churches everywhere. It's kind of like having your grandpa make all of your clothing decisions. There's going to be some inevitable conflicts (unless Mick Jagger is your grandpa). But there is also a direct correlation between the median age of a church and its odds of reaching unchurched people.

Researchers have known for a long time that most people who accept Christ do so at a young age. There have been dozens of researchers like George Barna who have shown that receptivity to the gospel decreases with age. Not surprisingly, numerous studies have also found that, as churches and their leaders age, their odds of both growing and reaching unchurched people plummets.[49]

Why? It's not rocket science. The vast majority of receptive, unchurched people are young. Yet, most churches tend to take on the median age of their prominent staff. Thus, as churches and their leaders age, they statistically tend to focus less on the youthful world of the unchurched. And if they do grow at all, these churches have a much higher likelihood of benefiting from transfer growth as opposed to unchurched growth.

Another reason why older churches grow less is because young people have this unique ability to create more babies than senior citizens. (Hopefully I don't have to

> *The vast majority of receptive, unchurched people are young.*

explain this.) Thus, churches with younger median ages also benefit from *procreation growth*—not just conversion growth.

Honestly, amidst all the flurry of church growth books, I'm surprised there aren't a few more pushing a procreation strategy. My book could be called *The Procreation-Driven Church*. Then I'd follow it up with a bestseller titled *The Procreation-Driven Life*. Come on, people! This is a rare moment in history when this could work. At the very least, growth goals would become way more entertaining. I always imagine our church logo with the slogan, "Be Fruitful and Multiply." Imagine a pastor standing up saying, "Can I get a hundred more men to stand up and pledge to making one more baby this year?" I suspect there would be a lot less men whining, "This church only cares about numbers."

With such a strategy, Catholics and Mormons would definitely have a theological advantage over evangelicals. We evangelicals would have to think creatively, like marriage retreats or more reality shows about large families like the Duggars. But, all jokes aside, this widening generation gap is actually the source of a huge amount of tension in Western churches.

Again, I don't want to keep depressing you, but check out the raw data: Numerous polls claim that 40 to 47 percent of Americans attend church. But we also know that people routinely lie about polling questions that make them feel guilty—such as how many people claimed to have voted but didn't. And, you thought Uncle Sam wasn't watching.

As I mentioned in the introduction, the most reliable research on the American church shows that far less people attend than we ever thought. Only 9.1 percent attend an evangelical or charismatic church on a weekly basis. In fact, there's not been a single state in the U.S. (except Hawaii) where church growth even kept up with population growth in over twenty years (since 1990)![50] Thus, suffice it to say, young people are quitting church as we know it.

So, the next question is this: *How can we stop this trend?* After talking with hundreds of dynamic young people about it, a few themes have emerged. So allow me to share a couple of *their* thoughts as to why.

Stuck at the Kids' Table

Recently, I was talking with a group of dynamic young leaders in our church, many of whom are around the age of twenty-five and leading some of our largest ministries. They all know that by twenty-four years old, I ran a ministry that had more than fourteen thousand attendees. Granted, I was only able to accomplish that because smarter leaders believed in me, so I wanted to return the favor by resourcing these leaders and holding the bar pretty high.

They kept saying to me, "Thanks for giving us a chance to truly impact this church." Of course, in my mind I didn't think I was doing anything special. So I finally asked them, "Why do you all keep saying that to me?" One of them finally responded, "In most churches, you can't even have a say on anything significant till you're at least forty years old—nor will you fit in until you're fifty. But here, you expect us to be leading large ministries by twenty-five. It's just inspiring!"

Another young leader proclaimed, "At my last church, they had a young adult service for people wanting 'edgier worship' on Saturday nights. And although their intensions were good, the mere existence of such a service felt like a death sentence, like forcing a twenty-nine-year-old to perpetually sit at the kids' table on Thanksgiving. So we finally left."

In other words, the whole philosophy of a youth-oriented service subtly communicated to this dynamic young man, "We don't want your influence, your music, or your culture in the main service." So naturally, he had a harder time taking ownership.

The truth is, these young people are not a minority anymore. Indeed, they represent the majority of America— not to mention the culture of America's most receptive unchurched population.

And don't get me wrong, relegating people toward young adult services or other non-ideal service times would make sense if we were talking about a minority demographic wanting a bizarre or esoteric worship style. But, the truth is, these young people are not a minority anymore. Indeed, they represent the majority of America—not to mention the culture of America's most receptive unchurched population.

It's no wonder they're cynical about a church that claims to be interested in the lost. They see a massive disparity between the church and the lost people churches claim to be reaching; yet, they simultaneously feel powerless to change any of it. Not surprisingly, young people have responded with a loud "See you later!" In fact, only 27 percent of Americans have any faith in the organized church—and that's the lowest it's been in the last forty years.[51] In other words, when you add up the small number of Christians under the age of twenty-nine who still attend church, it's rare to find one who isn't brimming with cynicism.

UNFURLING OUR MIDDLE-AGED GUTS

So what does Substance do differently to reach young people? Obviously, our church prefers to push the envelope when it comes to worship styles during Sunday services. For example, we have a DJ with turntables in most of our weekend bands. In the past, we've set some pretty unusual goals, such as having one rap-worship song per set. And, believe it or not, we're capable of doing an entire worship set in techno. We also do a lot with the creative digital arts. So, a lot of people expect me to be the "relevance will save the church" guy. But I'm not. In fact, many churches would be committing suicide by doing an all-techno set.

Don't get me wrong: There are a lot of churches that could afford to be a bit more in sync with the culture around them. The best-selling artist of the last *decade* (2000–2010) was the rap artist Eminem; yet, ironically, the majority of Christian leaders don't even know who he is—let alone listen to a single rap artist. So, yes, the cultural gap between the church and most Americans is still wider than ever. But the disparity isn't limited to music.

Young Americans also carry some extremely different assumptions about Scripture than previous generations.

Young Americans also carry some extremely different assumptions about Scripture than previous generations. Quite often, American pastors assume far too much about the biblical literacy of their audiences, or that they even believe in the Bible. Quite often, churches are obsessed with giving answers before stopping to ask young people if they have any questions.

Thus, many aging or cloistered Christians are like a doctor who shoves celery down the throats of people who are having heart attacks. Yes, those people probably should have been eating more celery, which would have prevented a heart attack in the first place, but we need to deal with the blockage first. And only after saving them can we teach them about how to eat healthier food. Likewise, attempting to disciple Christians who haven't even gotten basic things down—like consistent church attendance—is misguided and sometimes even foolish.

Thus, even if young Christians attend our churches, they're reticent to invite their friends out of fear we'll jam celery down their throats. They don't want to sound like they're against celery for fear of being viewed as compromised. Yet, they also don't want to jeopardize the investment they've poured into their non-Christian friends or coworkers. The following story serves as a perfect illustration.

KILLING PEOPLE WITH SPIRITUAL STEAK

A while back I remember hearing the story of a U.S. soldier who liberated a particular concentration camp in World War II Germany. The Jewish prisoners were virtually starved to death. So, in their zeal to help, the service men gave these starving prisoners large quantities of meat.

The sad part was that the frail bodies of these Jewish prisoners couldn't even digest it. And in the end, a huge number of them died because it was the wrong food at the wrong time.

I wish everyone could have seen the documentary film of this serviceman. He wept and wept because he realized that he was responsible for feeding these people the wrong food. And this is exactly what the apostle Paul was talking about when he rebuked the church in 1 Corinthians 14.

There was a good number of Corinthian Christians who thought that they were more spiritual than everyone else (1 Cor. 14:36). Earlier on, Paul warned them that their meetings do "more harm than good" (1 Cor. 11:17). Their "depth" was starting to freak people out, particularly when it came to unknown tongues.

Thus, Paul wrote, "I thank God that I speak in tongues more than any of you. But in a church meeting I would rather speak five understandable words to help others than ten thousand words in an unknown language. Dear brothers and sisters, don't be childish in your understanding of these things" (1 Cor. 14:18–20 NLT).

So, keeping the word *childish* in mind, let's skip down to verse 23, "So, if unbelievers or people who don't understand these things come into your church meeting and hear everyone speaking in an unknown language, they will think you are crazy." Thus, Paul encourages leaders to be wise about how they practice this.

But, the greater point here is this: There are legitimate spiritual experiences that certain people aren't ready for. So, once again, there's nothing wrong with "spiritual steak." It's fine to feed people deep teachings and spiritual experiences, but if you see someone jamming huge chunks of steak down a baby's throat, you darn well better

> *If you see someone jamming huge chunks of steak down a baby's throat, you darn well better rescue that baby.*

rescue that baby. Most people would call this child abuse. You don't feed a baby steak when they can only digest milk. It's Discipleship 101. But in many churches like the Corinthian church, these types of practices are actually deemed spiritual.

Although relevance is important to young people, authenticity is far more important.

So, the reason why Paul is calling them childish is because they fail to understand the process of discipleship. When pastors and leaders fail to realize the spiritual immaturity of our culture at large, it results in a grand-scale disaster. Christians yipe about the church lacking potency; yet, ironically, the misguided potency of certain churches is often amplifying the mortality rate. Even worse, the moment a church acknowledges this problem and makes adjustments, numerous cloistered Christians will immediately throw out the label of "compromise"—just as they did to Christ when He started rebuilding bridges.

So what do we do about this? Should we abandon meaty experiences? Absolutely not! Once young people experience God's power and grow past infancy, they're going to hunger for deep encounters with God's Word, even more than some adult Christians. But if pastors fail to delineate clear feeding stations, people will continue to fight over the purpose of the weekly church service.

And what about debates over relevant music and formats? Young people do not want to see more old people rapping like Marshall Mathers, nor do they want baby-boomers to unfurl their middle-aged guts to show off their new belly-button piercing. Although relevance is important to young people, authenticity is far more important.

And, beyond this, most young people are looking for something far more exhilarating: specifically, *ownership*. And why? Next to fellowship, ownership in the body of Christ is one of the most intoxicating experiences a church can offer.

THE POWER OF OWNERSHIP

Before I had kids, I had an aversion to holding babies. I simply had no interest in them. Part of it is that I have an aversion to bodily fluids (other than my own). I've been to the front lines, the place where diapers couldn't contain the decimation that awaited. And the few times I had to change another kid's diaper, it almost killed me.

But once I had kids of my own, everything changed. I'm not saying that I suddenly dove into the war on poop with patriotic enthusiasm, but ownership made a huge difference. And studies show that the same holds true with the church.

Back in 2004, there was a large study done comparing Christians who served in a church on a weekly basis to Christians who merely attended a church. And listen to what they found:

> *Those who volunteer at their church on a weekly basis are much more likely than non-volunteers to be satisfied with their church, with their spiritual lives, and in their relationship with God.*[52]

In other words, ministry ownership has a massive effect on three areas of a believer's life: church satisfaction; personal spiritual growth; and an ability to connect with God. These are some pretty amazing benefits! So, if we give a rip about people, we're going to make sure they have a meaningful place to serve.

Once again, this is exactly what the apostles were doing back in Acts 6. If you remember, there was a similar cultural gap forming in the early church. Grecian Jews were feeling marginalized by the Hebraic Jews. There was a representation problem in the church.

Rather than teaching baby boomers to dress younger and start rapping (a cheap-renovation approach), perhaps we need to start looking for more anointed young people to empower.

So what did the apostles do? They created the first multiethnic launch team alongside a disciple named Stephen. They balanced out their demographics by creating a leadership team that represented the group being overlooked.[53]

The American church would do well to apply a similar strategy. Rather than teaching baby boomers to dress younger and start rapping (a cheap-renovation approach), perhaps we need to start looking for more anointed young people to empower. If you can find young people like Stephen, who are "full of God's grace and power," chances are these young people will know how to reach their generation better than anyone.

FINDING THE FOUNTAIN OF YOUTH

Let me get practical by sharing some simple ways to apply this apostolic example:

1. Churches need to celebrate leaders on their platforms who represent their mission. Nothing says "We value your demographic" like giving young people strategic and visible positions in a church service.

2. Keep the median age of a church staff under forty years old. Keep in mind, the majority of receptive, unchurched people are young and multiethnic. So, this isn't an affirmative action ploy. It's a simple act of survival.

And remember, this doesn't devalue the role of older people. If anything, it will ultimately heighten their value. After all, once you fill up your church with meth addicts, sex addicts, and thirty-somethings with messed up marriages, you'll quickly see the need for healthy parental figures. Besides, deep down, most people simply want to be a part of a church that's truly growing and changing lives. And even if the youthfulness makes them uncomfortable, they will eventually become addicted to the fruit, even if that means playing a different role.

3. Allow the youth culture to define the main services. Churches like Hillsong have long been allowing their youth culture to define their primary services. Not surprisingly, they've been able to accomplish significant things in cities that many thought were church-planting graveyards, a term that's often attached to youthful cities.

But no matter what kind of church you attend, keep this in mind, "Big ships steer slowly." Be patient with your church. And don't burn your Aunt Suzi's Bible study group for not wanting to hear your new punk song in church.

Many of you may not even be in a position to affect these types of changes. If that's you, talk to your leaders in an honoring way. If you get the sense that the church is going in a different direction, graciously let the Lord lead you to a church that fits. But do not—I repeat, *do not*—lead a rebellion at your church. And, equally bad, don't become one of those cynical Christians who are so opinionated about church that you find yourself incompatible with every form of Christianity out there. Either way, you render yourself useless to the kingdom, which is the last thing God desires for you.

Although the Bride of Christ may have a few warts, don't let it stop you from falling in love. If you're a young person who feels disenchanted, reinvest yourself. If you're an older person who feels threatened, don't forget that spiritual grandchildren are one of the greatest pleasures God gives us in this life.

In the end, eternity is being determined by our every action in this life. And when we enter into heaven's worship, our biggest pleasure isn't going to be the music style or message format. Rather, it's going to be who we get to worship with (Dan. 12:2–3). So let's take as many people with us as we can.

> *"Big ships steer slowly." Be patient with your church.*

CHAPTER NINE IN REVIEW

Key Ideas

1. Christians who aren't regularly exposed to the messy lives of drug addicts and cohabiting couples lose their ability to see God's purpose for His church.

2. Cloistered Christians analyze and critique everything.

3. Cloistered churches become unhealthily self-oriented.

4. The vast majority of receptive unchurched people are young.

5. It's rare to find a Christian under twenty-nine who isn't brimming with cynicism.

6. American pastors assume far too much about the biblical literacy of their audiences.

7. Next to fellowship, ownership in the body of Christ is one of the most intoxicating experiences a church can offer.

8. Ministry ownership has a massive effect on three areas of a believer's life: church satisfaction; personal spiritual growth; and an ability to connect with God.

9. Churches need to celebrate leaders on their platforms who represent their mission.

10. Big ships steer slowly. Be patient with your church.

Discussion Questions

1. Were you surprised by the stat about median age affecting odds of reaching the unchurched? Why or why not? In your opinion, what are some practical ways this age gap is affecting the church at large, as well as yours specifically? Give a few examples.

2. Would you describe your church as cloistered or committed? Explain your response.

3. If self-orientation is an indicator of the spiritual health of your church, how healthy is your church? Explain your response.

4. Why are so many young Christians cynical? What can your church do to change their attitudes?

5. How would you describe the biblical literacy of the people in your church with whom you most often associate?

6. What type of music would you call relevant for your community? Would you consider yourself to be normative of your community? And do you think changes in worship music would really make a difference in reaching unchurched people? Why or why not?

7. We read that being involved in weekly ministry of a local church has a profound impact on people's church satisfaction as well as their relationships with God. In light of that, how does this affect your view of involvement in a church? Do you feel like you have an adequate amount of ownership in a local church?

8. What are some practical things that affect your involvement in a local church? And what types of things could you do to enhance your ownership?

9. Why is it important to grant ministry ownership to younger members of the Christian family?

10. In your opinion, what are some practical ways that Western churches could get more young people involved? And, are all churches capable of making those changes? Why or why not?

CONCLUSION

The Real Reason Religiously Diseased People Are Messed Up

What is it that truly reveals Christ to the World?

I'VE ALWAYS WANTED TO WRITE A book conclusion that includes something crazy like, "Therefore, all biblical Christians should do colon cleanses." That way, all of the people who skipped to the end (you know who you are) would be confused. The shortcutters would think, "Wow! I never saw that coming." Or at the very least, "It took nine chapters to conclude that?" And the rest of us would snicker.

I don't blame people for cutting to the chase. After all, so much of the world overflows with meaningless words. Those of us who are smart will look for the most important ones. And that's how I feel when I read the final words of Christ.

Toward the end of John's gospel, Jesus knew that His time was coming to a close. Christ knew that many of His disciples would soon be put to death by religiously diseased people. So He gave them a command that would undeniably set them apart: "A new command I give you: Love one another. . . . By this everyone will know that you are my disciples, if you love one another" (John 13:34–35).

It's almost strange that Jesus would call it new. It's bizarre to imagine that a joy-filled spiritual family of love would somehow be novel. Yet it reveals the spiritual landscape from which Christ sought to distinguish Himself. And I'm not convinced that the spiritual landscape of today is much different than that of Christ's time on earth.

Whether we like it or not, God says that a loving community is the single greatest revelatory attribute of His church.

Many modern church leaders would prefer to modify Jesus' command to: "Preach great Bible-based sermons, and by this all men will know . . ." But that's not what Jesus said. Still, others would modify God's Word to say, "Have deep prophetic worship experiences speckled with miracles, and by this all men will know . . ." Still others would modify God's Word to say, "Have relevant church services . . . and by this all men will know . . ."

And, yes, I believe these are important facets of healthy Christianity. Whether we like it or not, God says that a loving community is the single greatest revelatory attribute of His church. Yet, it's sermons and worship experiences and theological debates that modern-day Pharisees worry about most.

The real reason religiously diseased people fret over these things is because they ultimately don't believe that the grace of Jesus Christ is good enough. Their fears and insecurities drive them to numerous destructive behaviors. And here are a few that we covered in the first half of the book:

The real reason religiously diseased people fret over these things is because they ultimately don't believe that the grace of Jesus Christ is good enough.

- Religiously diseased people motivate themselves and others using guilt rather than kindness and grace (Titus 2:11–12; Matt. 13:44).

- Religiously diseased people proclaim truth outside of the context of loving friendship (1 Cor. 13:1; 1 Thess. 2:8).

- Religiously diseased people preach an obedience that comes from obligation rather than faith (Rom. 1:5–6).

- Religiously diseased people bid us to "take up crosses" without preaching a "joy set before us" (Heb. 12:2).

- Religiously diseased people want to be like God through the pursuit of the knowledge of good and evil (Gen. 3:5) when only the Christ of Scripture can make us like God (John 5:39–40). And He does this by living in us (Col. 1:27), not by our command of theology.

- Religiously diseased people find their identity in doctrines and methods, rather than in the one "who loved [us] and gave himself for [us]" (Gal. 2:20; Col. 3:3–4).

- Religiously diseased people create unity through uniformity of thought rather than through love.

CORPORATE SPIRITUAL DISEASES

You'll notice that most of the maladies mentioned above affect your personal experience of Christianity. I call them personal religious diseases. But as we moved into the latter half of the book, we discovered corporate religious diseases that have a much more profound effect on those around you. So here are a few other dysfunctional ideas that religiously diseased people engage in:

- They believe that the worship God delights in is a church-service format rather than a lifestyle or attitude of the heart (John 4:23). They even think that church-service formats are a measurement of the Holy Spirit.

- They think the church exists for Christians rather than for lost sheep (John 15). This leads them to value worship and sermon formats that coddle the righteous as opposed to help the sick (Mark 11:15).

- They think that church services are the summation of a church's gospel rather than a small slice of a greater whole. They believe they can tell if a church is Bible-believing or filled with the Spirit by its church services or sermons rather than the lifestyles or fruitfulness of its people (Matt. 7:16).

- They obsess over isolated purposes for God's church as though their narrow approaches outline the most spiritual way to be a Christian. Thus, they don't choose their church based on how balanced it is or how it stretches them. Rather, they choose it by how much it scratches their preferred gospel agenda. They conceal their crass consumerism under the false pretense of defending "pure" spirituality.

- They protect people by making gray areas of Scripture black and white. Or they create community rules as a shortcut to cultivating individual discernment, not realizing their protections become prisons (Acts 15:10).

No matter who you are, you will struggle with a few of these religious diseases throughout your life. No one is exempt. And you cannot combat religious diseases with cynicism, bitterness, or thoughtless critique. Ironically, those are the very ingredients that foster religious diseases in the first place.

That's why Peter echoed Christ's new command by saying: "Above all, love each other deeply, because love covers over a multitude of sins" (1 Peter 4:8). Peter knew that everyone makes mistakes, himself included. Eventually, someone else's sin is going to slap you in the face or make your life harder.

So remember this: The most accurate measure of your maturity is how well you react to another person's brokenness. The deeper your trust in Christ, the easier it is to remain an innocent child of God. And that's what I want for all of you.

The most accurate measure of your maturity is how well you react to another person's brokenness.

Life is too short to be bitter, wounded, or cynical. You may not come from a healthy church. You may not be able to make sense of the current pain in your life. But God can make sense of it all. He loves you, and He longs to make you a part of His family.

The church is not a perfect place. And quite often Christians do a terrible job at reflecting His true nature. Perhaps now you'll understand that our heavenly Father has His arms open wide—not because you have done all the right things, but because He has compassion on all He has made. And once we understand that it's not about us but Him living through us, there simply isn't anything left that can become diseased. Why? Because "you died, and your life is now hidden with Christ in God" (Col. 3:3).

So let's become Christ to the world. And then let's party for all eternity.

About the Author

ALTHOUGH ONLY IN HIS MID-THIRTIES, Pastor Peter Haas has already become a well-known pastor, author, and conference speaker. After experiencing a radical conversion to Christianity while working in a nightclub as a rave DJ, Peter has travelled the world sharing about God's miraculous passion.

After a decade of pastoring in Wisconsin, Peter and his family relocated to Minneapolis in 2004, planting an arts-oriented, multisite church called Substance (SubstanceChurch.com). In just a few short years, Substance has become one of the fastest-growing and most youthful megachurches in the United States. Over 70 percent of the thousands who participate in its community are younger than thirty years old. Known for its progressive worship, cell methods, and obvious appeal to unchurched twenty-somethings, Substance is making waves in the modern church world.

Peter consults with church planters all over the globe as he partners with the Association of Related Churches (ARC). With a unique blend of comedian, futurist, and Bible teacher, he regularly speaks at pastors' conferences and college events on topics ranging from spiritual growth to progressive church methods.

Beyond family and church, his next greatest passions are music, film, and stand-up comedy. He's an avid fan of indie rock. Playing just about every instrument, from cello to electric guitar, he spends most free nights in his recording studio, writing everything from electronica worship to classical film soundtracks.

Peter currently resides in Minneapolis with his wife, Carolyn, and their three kids. Visit PeterHaas.org or SubstanceChurch.com for his thoughts on church, life, theology, etc., and to download books, sermons, and other free resources. You may also follow him on Twitter (@PeterHaas1) as well as Facebook (Pastor Peter Haas).

Notes

1. Kirk Hadaway and Penny Marler's research estimates 20.4 percent. The American Church Research Project argues 17.5 percent. *http://www.hartfordinstitute.org/research/fastfacts/fast_facts. html#attend.*

2. David T. Olson, *The American Church in Crisis* (Grand Rapids, MI: Zondervan, 2008).

3. See *http://leadnet.org//blog/post/my_take_on_church_attendance_ and_the_nones*; or, check out: David Kinnaman, *You Lost Me: Why Young Christians Are Leaving Church and Rethinking the Faith* (Grand Rapids, MI: Baker Books, 2011).

4. Olson, *The American Church.*

5. We tend to see the Pharisees as the apex of legalism. Yet, many scholars argue that groups like the Sadducees were, in fact, more legalistic. For example, Pharisees were often accused of being "slippery" in their theology because of their acceptance of charismatic mysticism and a broader canon of Scripture. Pharisees also took a position on sovereignty theology that contemporaries often felt was "dangerously ambiguous" by refusing to subscribe to the predestination of the Essenes or the extreme free-will of the Sadducees. Ultimately, there are always exceptions to these stereotypes.

6. J. I. Packer, *Concise Theology* (Wheaton, IL: Tyndale House Publishers, Inc., 1993).

7. L. H. Powell, L. Shahabi, and C. E. Thoresen, "Religion and Spirituality: Linkages to Physical Health," *American Psychologist,* 58 (2003): 36–52.

8. A recent University of Chicago study known as "the most comprehensive and methodically sound sex survey ever conducted" found dramatically higher rates of "the Big O" in women who attend church services "religiously." This echoed a 1940s Stanford University Study and a 1970s *Red Book Magazine* survey that found higher levels of sexual satisfaction "among women who attend religious services religiously." Cited from William Mattox, Jr., "Aha! Call It the Revenge of the Church Ladies," *USA Today* (February 11, 1999).

9. In case you're not up on your biblical vocabulary, tithing is a biblical teaching of giving the first 10 percent of your income to your local church. Then, God supernaturally enables you to do more with your 90 percent than you were ever able to do with 100 percent (Mal. 3:10; Matt. 23:23; Prov. 3:9–10; Prov. 11:25–26). I realize that many people have felt abused by tithing teachings. If that's you, I'm really sorry. The disciples of the early church (those in the first two hundred years of the church) did, in fact, teach tithing as a starting point for new believers. However, they also taught it as a celebration, not an obligation. It was taught in a similar way as prayer. Prayer doesn't get you into heaven. It doesn't make God love you more. But, it clearly has supernatural implications. And it dramatically affects what your church is capable of doing. Also keep in mind that the average American church spends between six hundred and one thousand dollars per attender per year (that's primarily electricity, heating/AC, basic programming, and the cost of your chair). So, hopefully, you won't pull your heart or your finances back from God's work just because you've encountered a few lemon pastors.

10. See the site *www.globalrichlist.com* to see where your income lines up.

11. Dr. H. Norman Wright, renowned marriage and family therapist, found that "testing out a partner sexually" increases divorce odds to 75 percent; see *One Marriage Under God* (Sisters, OR: Multnomah Publishers, Inc., 2005).

12. See Jan E. Stets and Murray A. Straus, "The Marriage License As a Hitting License: A Comparison of Assaults in Dating, Cohabiting, and Married Couples," *Journal of Family Violence,* vol. 4, no. 2 (1989): 39; see also *http://www.eric.ed.gov/PDFS/ED296193.pdf (1988;* accessed 2012).

13. *Ibid.*

14. Wright, *One Marriage Under God,* 100.

15. A study quoted by Linda J. Waite and Maggie Gallagher, *Talk* (October 2000): 155.

16. A 1982 UCLA study and a University of Connecticut study found that non-religious women felt greater inhibition due to a feeling of increased sexual risks (e.g., fear of contracting STDs, etc.).

17. Reported by David Larson of the National Institute for Health Care Research.

18. This idea was given to me years ago by a pastor named Jess Strickland. So simple, yet profound.

19. See D. Michael Lindsay/Gallup Research, *Friendship: Creating a Culture of Connectivity in Your Church* (Loveland, CO: Group Publishing, Inc., 2005).

20. One of the largest church health and growth studies ever found that "holistic small groups" within a church have a profound effect. See Christian Schwartz, Natural Church Development (Saint Charles, IL: Churchsmart Resoruces, 1996). This syncs quite well with Michael Lindsay's friendship study in 2004. Ironically, church size has little to do with church intimacy and odds of authentic relational health.

21. E. A. Colon, A. L. Callies, M. K. Popkin, and P. B. McGlave, *Psychosomatics* (1991): 32, 420–25. For further examples, see Will Miller, Ph.D., *Refrigerator Rights* (New York, NY: The Berkley Publishing Group, 2002), 137–43.

22. Jolanda Jetten, Catherine Haslam, S. Alexander Haslam, and Nyla R. Branscombe, "The Social Cure," *Scientific American Mind,* (October 2009): 28.

23. J. Lynch, *The Broken Heart: The Medical Consequences of Loneliness* (New York: Basic Books, 1977), 239–42. See also Augustine J. Kposowa, "Marital Status and Suicide in the National Longitudinal Mortality Study," *Journal of Epidemiology and Community Health*, 54 (2000): 254–61.

24. Jetten, Haslam, Branscome, "The Social Cure": 28.

25. Jonah Lehrer, "The Buddy System: How the Medical Data Revealed Secret to Health and Happiness," *Wired Magazine*, Issue 17.10 (2009), 1.

26. *Ibid.*

27. *Hardwired to Connect: The New Scientific Case for Authoritative Communities*, a report to the nation from the Commission on Children at Risk, published by the Institute for American Values (2003), 19.

28. Although we snicker about this story as though it was an overreaction, I'm sure it was a bigger deal back then.

29. Some scholars estimate that 12 legions equaled about 72,000. That's a lot of angels.

30. Lindsay, *Friendship.*

31. For one example, see Lindsay, *Friendship.*

32. See Christian Schwartz, "Quality Characteristic #6," from the classic church growth book *Natural Church Development.*

33. See Lindsay, *Friendship.*

34. Olson, *The American Church.*

35. Sources: Elizabeth Cornelio, Brian Mills of *Interprayer,* and Hildegard Schneider of Bad Nauheim. Reported in *Friday Fax* #9, 26, and 37 (1999) as cited by James Rutz in *Mega Shift,* (Colorado Springs, CO: Empowerment Press, 2005), 70.

36. Although Augustine is often credited with saying this, Rupertus Meldenius is usually the individual that scholars credit (circa 1627).

37. There are many varieties of models illustrating "theological stratification." One of my favorite alternatives is the diagram found in the book *Your Primary Purpose* by Ted Haggard (Lake Mary, FL: Charisma House, 2006), 35–44. Some of the ideas here were influenced by Haggard's model.

38. For example, in 1 Corinthians 14:34, Paul wrote that women should be silent. However, in the context, he's also telling all sorts of other groups to be silent under certain circumstances, from tongue talkers to prophets. Also, we see in the book of Acts that Paul happily works with female prophets. In other places we see Paul giving instructions to female prophets. So, when Paul says that women should be "silent," is this a statement about how God universally designed women, or is it simply instruction to another group that needs to understand when speaking is appropriate (like tongue talkers and prophets)? In order to answer this, we must bring our assumptions to the text, as well as decide what to do with the other texts that confirm or deny such inferences.

39. For example, most speculations, such as arguments about predestination or free will, require us to answer questions that go beyond Scripture—such as *How literally or figuratively do we interpret certain passages of Scripture?* or *Who determines when we apply a literal or figurative approach to interpretation?* Even then, speculations require us to add numerous inferences together: A + B + C + D = Your Speculation.

40. Robert Epstein citing Barbara Morrongiello's University of Guelph study "What Makes a Good Parent," *Scientific American Mind,* (November/December 2010): 49.

41. Lindsay, *Friendship.*

42. This example is classic "family systems theory." For more, read Edwin H. Friedman's brilliant treatise, *Failure of Nerve* (New York, NY: Seabury Books, 2007).

43. Numerous studies confirm similar results for churches between years fifteen to twenty. For examples of such studies, see Win Arn, *The Pastor's Manual for Effective Ministry* (Monrovia, CA: Church Growth, 1988), 41; or "Churches Die with Dignity," *Christianity Today* (January 14, 1991): 69; or Olson, *The American Church.*

44. Lindsay, *Friendship.*

45. Churches with free-market cells (affinity-based ministry groups) have greater ministry opportunities that sync with people's gift mixes and passions. For example, see Schwartz, Quality Characteristic #2, *Natural Church Development.*

46. As one example, see Daniel Goleman, Annie McKee, and Richard E. Boyatzis, *Primal Leadership: Realizing the Power of Emotional Intelligence* (Boston: Harvard Business School Publishing, 2002), 7, 10.

47. Schwartz, Quality Characteristic #8, *Natural Church Development.*

48. For an expanded version of this story, see Billy Hornsby, *The Attractional Church: Growth Through a Refreshing, Relational, and Relevant Church Experience* (Nashville, TN: FaithWords, 2011), 22–24.

49. Olson, *The American Church.*

50. *Ibid.*

51. This number comes from a 2007 Harris Poll.

52. Lindsay, *Friendship.*

53. It's critical to note that they all had Grecian names.

To Order More
Copies of This Book

Pharisectomy is available online at

www.InfluenceResources.com

where group discounts are available.

You can also buy this book
at Christian bookstores and
e-book retailers.